MORE BAD GIRLS OF THE BIBLE

More
Bad Girls
of the Bible

Barbara J. Essex

THE PILGRIM PRESS
CLEVELAND

Dedication

To the memory of one my dearest friends,

Quinn Alice Robinson Carter

A pillar of strength and courage . . .

"I love you, girl!"

The Pilgrim Press, 700 Prospect Avenue, Cleveland, Ohio 44115,
www.thepilgrimpress.com
© 2009 by Barbara J. Essex

Printed in the United States of America on acid-free paper.

14   13   12   11   10   09   5   4   3   2

Library of Congress Cataloging-in-Publication Data

Essex, Barbara J. (Barbara Jean), 1951–
    More bad girls of the Bible / Barbara J. Essex.
    p. cm.
    ISBN 978-0-8298-1824-6 (alk. paper)
    1. Women in the Bible.   2. Bible—Commentaries.   I. Title.
BS575.E88 2009
220.9'2082—dc22   2008046297

Contents

GETTING STARTED

This Bible study consists of twelve units and is designed for individual and/or group study. Leaders do not need extensive small group training. Each study unit begins with a focus text and a review of the stories of selected biblical women. A short commentary follows, which provides background information to help make the story understandable and raises issues for consideration. Each unit ends with reflection questions to help start a discussion about what we can learn from these characters and their stories. This book is designed to help us examine our own motives, assumptions, and identity as we explore the stories of our faith.

Try to allow one and a half to two hours for each unit; feel free, however, to make adjustments that work for you or your group. The materials you need include this book, a Bible in a version with which you are comfortable, and a notebook or journal in which to record your answers and reflections.

A suggested format for group study is:

- Assign readings ahead of time—the scripture as well as the unit to be studied.

- If necessary, set some "ground rules" for the discussion (for example, everyone will have an opportunity to voice his/her opinion without judgment from other group members; no one needs to agree with everyone else; one person speaks at a time; no name calling; etc.)

- Begin each session with a prayer for open minds and meaningful discussion.

- Review the information in the study unit; answer any questions.

- Use the reflection questions at the end of each unit to start the discussion or generate your own questions.

- Share insights about the text, as much as people feel comfortable with sharing.

- Assign the next unit.

- Close with prayer.

If you are using this resource for personal study, you should still allow one and a half to two hours for each study unit. You will need a journal in which to record your reflections and questions.

At the end of this book, you will find a section with suggestions for preaching and teaching about these bad girls. The bibliography and resources section lists additional books, articles, and websites that you may find helpful as you continue your studies. Of course, you should include any resources you find helpful to supplement the lessons here.

I encourage you to have fun; there is much to learn about these biblical folks as well as about ourselves. I hope that these study units will help you answers some questions you may have about the Bible and your faith. Most of all, I hope you find these studies to be informative, challenging, and inspirational. Enjoy your journey.

ACKNOWLEDGMENTS

Every book springs from a thought, a challenge, a question, a vision, a hope—I have been encouraged by a host of folks to write this volume as a continuing exploration to the first *Bad Girls of the Bible: Exploring Women of Questionable Virtue.* I offer my gratitude to women and men who have asked about women not included in the first volume—summer classes at Catholic Theological Union (Chicago) and Pacific School of Religion (Berkeley); congregational groups from Maine to Canada to Connecticut to North Carolina to Illinois to Texas to California; Bible study sessions across denominational lines—United Church of Christ, African Methodist Episcopal, United Methodist, Presbyterian, Christian Church (Disciples of Christ), and Baptist; and conversation partners who nudge and push me to continue writing and teaching.

I continue to thank God for those who support me in this writing endeavor: Kim Martin Sadler, Michael Lawrence, and their colleagues and partners at The Pilgrim Press.

I am grateful for my family and friends who provide unconditional support, love, and interest in what keeps me so isolated at times—Patricia Essex, Ta-Tanisha Essex, Brenda Fluker, Linda Sroufe, Carolyn Young, O'Weedy Mitchell, Belinda Bell, Valerie Deering, Linda Mines, Cynthia Baines, Opal Easter, and my friend Quinn Carter, who died in March 2008. I always get by with a little help from my friends and I feel so blessed.

I am grateful, too, for pastors and clergy who trusted me to share these bad girls with their congregations and who have provided extended teaching opportunities: J. Alfred Smith Sr., Brenda Guess, Kelvin Sauls, Charie Reid, Denise Burroughs, and a host of others.

A special thanks to staff, students, recent graduates, and faculty at Pacific School of Religion who continue to show interest in my work and who provide comic relief and time-outs just when I need them—Ann Jefferson, Marjorie Wilkes, Terry Dyonzak, Nina Galvan, Ada Renee Williams, Donnel Miller-Mutia, Jeremy Gameros, Archie Smith Jr., Joe Driskill, D. Mark Wilson, Niccole Coggins, Adriene Thorne, Lavon Stalling, Emily Joye McGaughey, Kim Montenegro, and Gayle Basten.

I owe a lifetime of gratitude to my mentors and teachers who opened the depths of the Bible and made it real for me: Jeremiah A. Wright Jr., Carl Marbury, S. Dean McBride, Ernest T. Campbell, George Polk, and Thomas Hoyt Jr.

Finally, any strength of this volume is due to input from all who challenged and critiqued my thinking and research. All weaknesses are due to my own inadequacies.

INTRODUCTION

My seminary preaching professor, Ernest T. Campbell, asked why I am so preoccupied with sin. His query came on the heels of the publication of *Misbehavin' Monarchs*, the fifth in a series, that looks at the strengths and weaknesses of biblical rulers and power brokers. The preaching of my pastor, Jeremiah A. Wright Jr., at Trinity United Church of Christ, set the tone for me—he did not sugarcoat the humanity of those who help us understand who God is and what God is up to in the world. Once I started looking at the triumphs and tragedies of biblical characters, I just couldn't stop—sin is fun! Well, the consequences are not fun, but pointing out the sins of biblical personalities allows us to connect with and learn from them. I feel compelled to help us get a fuller picture of those folks we preach about and hold up as paragons of faith and faithfulness.

Ten years ago, *Bad Girls of the Bible: Exploring Women of Questionable Virtue* was published. I had no idea how much attention the volume would garner—study groups, sermon series, retreat themes, Bible study sessions, seminary classes—it seems that folks just love bad girls. There are "Bad Girls" groups across the country who meet on a regular basis. More and more churchwomen across denominations, ages, class, and race are identifying themselves as bad girls—with smiles, pride, attitude, and activism in their churches and communities. Even men have joined in on the fun of it all. And the secular world has taken to this image—there is a reality show and a series of books, calendars, and meditation cards with the Bad Girls label.

What accounts for the early and ongoing interest in bad girls? My interest goes back over twenty years to when the move to recover the stories of biblical women was just gaining momentum. My initial aim was to lift up some women in the Bible we love to hate to see what we could learn about them if we stripped away the patriarchal layers of judgment and condemnation. I also wanted us to consider how these women, named and unnamed, though considered to be shameful and shamed, disgraceful and disgraced, could be preached and taught in our congregations. I believed, and still do, that the bad girls should stand alongside the pillars of our faith—Abraham, Moses, Joshua, David, Elijah, Peter, Paul, James, and John. The bad girls embody values and perspectives that will serve us in the twenty-first century.

Over the past ten years, I have been positively challenged by women and men to write another volume—they said other bad girls were seeking to be seen and heard. And so here we are. Even this volume will not give voice to all the bad girls in the Bible . . . perhaps, there will be a volume three! Since the publication of *Bad Girls of the Bible*, there has been an explosion of books related to women's stories. I am happy to be among many others—women and men, scholars and pastors—who seek to open the riches of the Bible to women and men who seek ways to deepen their faith and have some fun doing so.

While I call the women in this book "bad girls," we know that they are a blend of both positive and negative qualities. In other words, they exhibit human characteristics and we can learn from them. In our preaching and teaching, we sometimes are so quick to highlight their flaws and sins that we fail to see positive, affirming, and life-giving lessons they have for us. The stories of women in the Bible are most often embedded in men's stories and serve as means to ends that support God's purpose and intentions. Some seemed destined to move the gospel story along by what they do or fail to do. Some will reflect back to us our own flaws, foibles, imperfections, and questionable choices. Rather than wallow in guilt or preach damnation, I hope that we can acknowledge those less than lovely aspects of our own personalities mirrored in the stories of the bad girls—some call us to repentance and improvement. I hope, also, that we are moved to greater compassion and service on behalf of humanity. Finally, I hope we are reminded that God's grace and mercy are abundant and available to each of us as we deal with the realities of our various contexts and as we make decisions and choices. I have chosen twelve women to study this time around; some are familiar to us and others are not.

In the Hebrew Bible, also known as the Old Testament, God called Abraham to come out of retirement and journey to a place that would be shown to him. Because of Abraham's faithful obedience, God established a covenant with him, promising progeny and prosperity. The road to a promised land and nationhood was filled with obstacles, detours, and delays—the story is dramatic and filled with miracles, tragedies, poor choices, and breached promises. Ultimately, the Assyrians and Babylonians destroyed the community God sought to establish through the Israelites after a golden age of power and prestige under the leadership of David and Solomon. From the Hebrew Bible, we explore the stories of Hagar, Shiphrah, Puah, Miriam, Zipporah, Bathsheba, Rizpah, and Huldah. They represent wives, mothers, midwives, sisters, performing artists, and prophets. Their stories showcase women's power in the midst of oppressive patriarchy, growth in the midst of repression, and ingenuity in the midst of debilitating social policies. They exercised power, subversive rebellion, creative expression, quick thinking, the claiming of voice, and action. These women were complex and spiritual beings whose stories teach us something about God and God's dealings with women in patriarchal cultures. They found ways to overcome social limitations and to make a difference within their spheres of influence. These women are named and we hear their words and watch their actions.

In the Christian Scripture, God tries again to bring God's people into community. After the powerful preaching and missionary work of John the Baptist, God empowered and anointed Jesus to continue the work of Moses, the monarchs, and the prophets of the Hebrew Bible. As the Messiah, Jesus worked hard to prepare the people for God's reign, challenging their thinking and values. After his death and resurrection, Jesus became the Christ of faith for Christians and the early church was born. The work of the early church continues into this twenty-first century—work that is sometimes exemplary and at times dismal and depressing. Here, too, we find some colorful characters with a few bad girls sprinkled in: Martha and Mary, Mary Magdalene, and some unnamed women—the bent-over woman, the Samaritan woman at the well, the Syrophoenician woman. These women are included because of their interactions with Jesus—they were active, witty, intelligent, believing women who show us what encounters with Jesus can lead to: greater and deeper faith, new theological understandings, new power and wholeness. They represent women who had encounters with Jesus that changed their lives and his. Their stories represent theological savvy, quick thinking, and the reframing of theological and missional understandings.

And why are these women labeled "bad girls"? The word "bad" is a relative term and doesn't mean that the biblical character is deficient. These women's stories require more than a surface reading. Some are considered "bad" because of their actions and the positions they found themselves in; for example, Rizpah was bad because of her silent vigil that so disturbed David that he had to do something he had no intention of doing—bring Saul and Jonathan's bones home to be buried, as well as those of the seven he gave up to ritual execution. In the text, Rizpah never utters a word and disappears when the men are properly buried. But she changed the course of action of the story because of her courageous action, whether intentional or not.

The "crippled/bent-over woman" can be seen as a foil in the power struggle between Jesus and his opponents; Jesus dared to heal her on the Sabbath. Yet her response was to praise God, which she was doing before her healing. The bottom line of her story is that whether sick or well, infirm or whole, praising God is the response for believers. Good news for some; not so good news for others, especially those who opposed Jesus and his realm of God movement. That Jesus healed a woman—a sick woman considered unclean and a nobody, expendable—was reason enough to be up in arms. She symbolizes women (and men) who are marginalized for no fault of their own; her story exposes the systems and structures, powers and principalities that would keep certain sectors of people oppressed, neglected, ignored. Her presence and response make her a "bad" girl.

The point of designating these women as "bad" is to show: (1) their very human sides; (2) their very courageous and outrageous sides; (3) the patriarchal layers that need to be stripped away to uncover admirable/positive qualities; (4) how God can take any situation and bring something good out of it; and (5) how these women can inspire and teach us valuable lessons today.

As we study the stories of these twelve women, we discover new insights about God and ourselves. Their stories help us to see our own stories and to see how God continues to deal with God's people. The bottom line is that God is still up to something in the world. When we think we have hit our lowest, something miraculous happens and keeps on happening. God is not done with us yet. This is good news for the bad girls who keep on keeping on.

Some of the units will present us with challenges—we might be reluctant to analyze closely the biblical women for fear that we will offend God. We might be confronted with information that seems blasphemous. We might be tempted to reject the possible lessons available to us. We might simply refuse to believe what is written. Critical study should deepen, broaden, and expand our faith as we learn more about who these characters were and what they can teach us. We are blessed to have sacred texts that give us pictures of real people who were not one-dimensional even when the biblical texts seem to provide flat portraits. We will see the good, the bad, and the ugly—the Bible does not present perfect people.

Well, we've plied these waters before—let's continue the journey.

I

HAGAR
Will God Make a Way, Somehow?

READ

Genesis 16:1–15, 21:8–21

FOCUS TEXTS

And [the angel of YHWH] said, "Hagar, slave-girl of Sarai, where have you come from and where are you going?" (Gen. 16:8)

[A]nd the angel of God called to Hagar from heaven, and said to her, "What troubles you, Hagar? . . ." (Gen. 21:17)

"Through it all, I've learned to trust in God; but going with the flow is not an easy thing!" By reading the selected biblical texts, we might be left to conclude that Hagar's only claim to fame is her victimization. In both texts, Abraham's wife, Sarah, casts her out of Abraham's household. Hagar seems to have no recourse or resources to manage her life and is at the mercy of a woman who uses her and then tosses her aside. But there is more to Hagar's story than meets the eye.

Hagar is a familiar figure in the black church tradition and the Islamic faith. For black Americans, she is the centerpiece for womanist theology and thought. For Muslims, she is the mother of the faith, and her son, Ishmael, as the firstborn son of Abraham, is a founding ancestor for the faith. We will look at both of these aspects of her story later in this chapter.

Hagar's story is embedded in the story of Abraham. She was part of a triangular relationship that included Abraham and his wife Sarah. Sarah, married to a man to whom God has promised progeny, was nevertheless barren. Infertility in ancient days was a serious condition. In Sarah's case, as for other biblical women, God had "closed" her womb and the fulfillment of God's promise to Abraham was in jeopardy. Her barrenness was no small matter for her or Abraham—the very life of a people depended on Abraham's capacity to father children, preferably sons, since the family line was passed through sons rather than daughters. Childlessness in those days was cause for shame and danger—the future could end if a woman was unable to give birth.

When we first meet her, Hagar is the Egyptian slave girl of Sarah, possibly part of Pharaoh's gifts to Abraham during his time in Egypt when he tried to deceive Pharaoh by pretending Sarah was not his wife but rather his sister only (see Gen. 12:10ff). Hagar could have been one of Sarah's servants while she lived in Pharaoh's palace, and Sarah was allowed to keep her. The text is very clear about identifying her in an inferior position to both Sarah and Abraham—she is an unmarried woman, a foreigner, and a slave. In contemporary terms, she is a victim of sexism, racism, and classism. Hagar belongs to Sarah and is under her complete control.

When the barren Sarah suggests that Abraham father a child with Hagar, she follows the customary and accepted method of providing a surrogate. Because Hagar is her property, Sarah is the legal parent of any children produced by

Hagar and Abraham. Abraham does not question Sarah's plan and complies. The text explains that Sarah "gives" Hagar to Abraham "as a wife" (Gen. 16:3b) in the same manner that a father gives his daughter to be married. In this instance, Hagar has no choice but to comply. She becomes Abraham's secondary wife.

In due time, Hagar becomes pregnant and her attitude towards Sarah changes. The text says that Hagar "looked with contempt on her mistress." In other words, Hagar realizes that she is now the superior one because she will bear the child of promise. But Sarah is not about to take any attitude from Hagar—Hagar is still a slave even though she is pregnant.

After consulting her husband, Sarah continued to take matters into her own hands and "dealt harshly" with Hagar. The Hebrew term used in the text is the same used of the Egyptians in their handling of their Israelite slaves. Rather than stay and take the abuse, Hagar runs away; yes, she is a runaway slave. Neither women try to work things out and are reactionary—Sarah reacts to Hagar's change of attitude and Hagar reacts to Sarah's abuse.

Hagar's intention is to return home to Egypt—at least there, she will be surrounded by familiar faces, possibly family and friends, and will know she belongs. She makes it over halfway home, to the spring in the desert of Shur, near the northeast border of Egypt. As it is now, she is homeless and without means of support. She is vulnerable to the elements as well as wild animals and bandits. She is in the wilderness where there are few resources for survival—little shade from the sun, little water to be found, few places of hospitality. Hagar is pregnant, a risky condition in ancient times. Women were always at risk for difficult pregnancies and complicated deliveries. Being in the wilderness certainly does not help her situation—the very question of her survival and that of her unborn child is paramount. Yet in the midst of her despair and the uncertainty of her future, she is visited by "the angel of YHWH," whom most scholars agree is the presence of God in human form. Although she knows she is encountering God, Hagar has no response to the poignant questions asked—she can only say where she's been. Hagar has no idea where she is headed, especially since it is not clear to her if she will even survive the trip.

The command for her to return to Abraham's house and Sarah's abuse is one that troubles scholars and should trouble us as well. Why is she being sent back into a situation of abuse? Why didn't Abraham intervene before she had to run away? Why does God condone and encourage the mistreatment of Hagar?

While the text raises questions, it also sets forth some fascinating points to ponder. Hagar's story is unusual in that she has agency—that is, she has the capacity to make choices and decisions. She runs away when the abuse is too much, even though she does so without adequate resources. She has voice and can articulate where she's been, even though she cannot say where she is going. She tries to take charge of her life and that of her unborn child. In her exchange with God, Hagar is given a promise that parallels that given to Abraham:

> Now [YHWH] said to [Abraham] "Go from your country and your kindred and your father's house to the land that I will show you. I will make of you a great nation, and I will bless you, and make your name great, so that you will be a blessing. I will bless those who bless you, and the one who curses you I will curse; and in you all the families of the earth shall be blessed." (Gen. 12:1–3)

And the angel of [YHWH] said to her,
> "Now you have conceived and shall bear a son;
> you shall call him Ishmael,
> for [YHWH] has given heed to your affliction.

He shall be a wild ass of a man,
   with his hand against everyone,
   and everyone's hand against him;
      and he shall live at odds with all his kin."
                                          (Gen. 16:11–12)

It seems that Hagar is reluctant to return to Abraham's household—and who can blame her? It is foolish for her to go back to a place that holds so much pain—physical, mental, emotional—and to know that she is not wanted there. She is either foolish or naïve to even consider going back—but God entices her with some perks: a roof over her head until her baby is born and a promise for her through her son. Now that's something worth going back for—women in ancient days depended on men for their livelihood and survival. To know that her son will inherit a promise, apart from Abraham, is something Hagar has to consider. If she doesn't, she will be in bad shape. The incentives work and she prepares to go back to Abraham and Sarah's home.

Hagar's story takes another interesting turn when she speaks in response to her encounter with God. She is the first in the Bible to name God: *El-roi*, the "God of seeing" or "God who sees." The implications of these actions are huge —an unmarried, foreign, slave woman converses with the God of Israel and names the deity. Some have suggested that the description of Ishmael and his future is unflattering; however, the qualities of determination, strength, and valor will serve him well as he makes his home in the desert, wilderness places of the Middle East.

With the divine promise held close to her heart, Hagar returns to Sarah's house despite the horrendous situation of abuse. We don't know how Hagar approaches Abraham and Sarah—what does she say? How is her demeanor—is she quiet, demure, humble? How does Sarah react seeing the bane of her existence back at her tent? Does Sarah welcome her or does she walk away? And what of Abraham—what does he do in this difficult situation? Does he apologize to Hagar? Does he try further to placate Sarah? The text does not give us any juicy details about the tensions in the household after Hagar's return. We know that she is taken back in and her life plays out just as the angel of God predicted—she bears a son whose name is Ishmael.

Things seem to roll right along—we imagine that Hagar is a good, caring, loving mother. We suspect that she does all she can to shield her son from Sarah for fear that the older woman will abuse the child. We hope that Abraham is a real father to the child and provides the love that a child wants from a parent. We can only surmise because the text is silent about what happens behind the closed doors of the Abraham home.

We next meet Hagar in Genesis 21 after Sarah has given birth to Isaac. God has done the impossible; Sarah, way past her prime and postmenopausal, becomes pregnant. How did she tell Abraham and how did Hagar find out? Sarah, no doubt astonished and pleased, likely is filled with joy. But her good news is probably not so good for Hagar. Sarah laughs at the mere suggestion that she might conceive. While Sarah laughs, Hagar weeps. While Sarah celebrates, Hagar shudders. While surprised and supportive friends surround Sarah, Hagar wonders if her days are numbered in the Abraham house. While Sarah's belly grows, Hagar's world shrinks. The issues between Sarah and Hagar are never resolved and the two women continue to live in tension with each other. The text is silent about Abraham and Ishmael and we are left to assume that, for them, all is right with the world.

We are not told what kind of mother Hagar is or what kind of stepmother Sarah is. We don't know how the tensions play out in this dysfunctional home. We are tempted to conclude that not much has changed. What is interesting to note is that now Hagar is referred to as the "Egyptian" and not the "Egyptian slave girl." Her status has changed because she is now also a mother. Despite the biblical story-teller's elevation of Hagar, Sarah continues to view her as a slave. All of her references to Hagar include her slave status. Even God seems stuck on her slave status and labels her as such when God speaks to Abraham about the ongoing dissension in the household.

This time, Sarah demands that Abraham send Hagar and her son away. The whole blended family thing is not working for Sarah. She does not want to share her life or her son's inheritance with Ishmael. Finally, we get a reaction from Abraham. He is distressed about sending his son, his first-born, away, implying genuine affection for the boy. He seems to love Ishmael and pleads with God to make Ishmael the son of promise (see Gen. 17:18). But even God repudiates Ishmael (see Gen. 17:19). Only incidentally are Abraham and God concerned about Hagar. In the face of rejection and indifference (again), God continues to say that things will be all right for Hagar and Ishmael. God reiterates the promise given to Hagar about Ishmael's future (see Gen. 21:11–13). With the assurance that his second wife and first son will be okay, Abraham sends his family away into the wilderness. Both Hagar and Ishmael must deal with being unwanted and despised.

Again, God visits Hagar in the wilderness and asks a probing question—"What troubles you, Hagar?" Instead of answering, she lifts her voice to weep. Where should she begin? She has a catalog of ills—we wonder if Sarah continued to abuse her and if Sarah abused Ishmael in any way. We know that both Abraham and Sarah continue to view her as a slave, so in their eyes Hagar's status has not really changed. As tears gush from her eyes and before she can control the anguished sounds from her throat, God provides the resources for her survival and that of her son. Once more, God assures Hagar that things will work out (see Gen. 21:18). In this episode, instead of a strong, defiant woman with an attitude, we see an overwhelmed, emotional wreck of a mother. We wonder if nearly sixteen years of stress have taken their toll on Hagar. In Genesis 16, she has voice and agency; here in Genesis 21, she is reduced to weeping and wailing. In the earlier passage, she leaves on her own accord; here she is cast out. It is not clear if her words in Genesis 21:16b are verbal or her silent thoughts. Once again, God provides for Hagar and her child.

Ishmael grows up, Hagar finds a wife for him from among their people (Egyptians), he returns to help Isaac bury their father, and he lives to see God's promise fulfilled. Hagar disappears from the text—we don't know when or how she died, nor do we know where she is buried.

The story of Hagar raises a number of theological and ethical questions about God's dealings with her, about Abraham's dealings with her, and certainly about Sarah's dealings with her. None of these characters shine in these episodes with Hagar. God seems to condone abuse, is willing to send her back into a situation where her well-being is in jeopardy—ironically, though God provides for her survival, Hagar is still told to return to Sarah's house. Abraham stands by passively as Sarah abuses and mistreats the mother of his firstborn child. In these texts, Sarah is mean, vindictive, and brutal. Hagar seems like a victim of all three—Sarah, Abraham, and God.

We are left to wonder if Hagar's story is only about victimization:

- Her status as a slave, and a foreign one, means she has no rights anyone in Abraham's camp is obligated to acknowledge or respect. Hagar is basically a nobody in Abraham's household. Her story raises questions about who is valued, and on what basis that value is assessed. Knowing how it feels to be rejected and abused, Hagar sees no alternative except to run away. What she cannot see, God sees all too well, as Hagar will find out.

- She has no say in whether she is willing to have sex with Abraham or to bear his child. She is handed over by Sarah, who has the right to do so; Hagar's resistance is not a possibility or option. But Sarah sees Hagar as a rival despite her power over Hagar.

- Hagar's status changes with the birth of her son. Hagar is expendable but the son is not. She has the possibility, now, of a future because Ishmael is Abraham's legal heir. In addition, sons are obligated to care for their mothers if the fathers precede them in death. But Hagar doesn't have the last word in her own story—Sarah does by having Hagar sent away.

We notice that in the texts where Hagar appears, no one speaks directly to her except God. Neither Sarah nor Abraham addresses her in the texts. They don't give a hoot about her except in terms of what she can do to enhance their lives. While she is a mere commodity for the husband and wife, Hagar is somebody in God's eyes. God speaks to her and calls her by name.

Hagar's life hinges on decisions made by others. Sarah treats her cruelly, while Abraham takes a hands-off approach to the domestic situation except to impregnate her. Hagar's future is uncertain and unpredictable. God promises her a future that is tied to the successful birth of a son. It is difficult to see how God will pull this miracle off by sending her back into the abusive household from which she has fled. Even after the birth of her son, Hagar wanders again in the wilderness—the same wilderness the Israelites will wander under Moses, Miriam, and Aaron.

In the Hebrew context, wilderness (in Hebrew, *midbar*) is a scary, isolated, dangerous place. The term serves as a metaphor for places of desolation that are chaotic and hazardous. Twice Hagar is in the wilderness—without shelter, food, water, or protection. Both times, she is vulnerable and her future is uncertain, first as a pregnant woman and second as a mother with a teenage child. What chance does she have when others are determining her fate?

Lots of questions, to be sure. But our questions do not form the conclusion of Hagar's story. Even though she seems to be a victim, Hagar has enough self-awareness to know when it is time to leave Abraham's house. She has enough self-esteem to know that her status of slave has changed with her pregnancy. Her independent streak kicks in to let her know when enough is enough. She is humble enough to comply with God's command that she return to Abraham and Sarah for the sake of the child—and savvy enough to wait until the benefits are explained. And she is able to deliver a healthy son upon whom God places a divine promise.

When at her lowest, she is visited by God, who finds her, calls her by name, and makes a way for her to keep on keeping on. God, who seems to condone abuse and violence, nonetheless hears and sees Hagar, responds to her situation, and points her to the future.

There is tremendous hope in Hagar's story despite all the odds against her—God continues to show up. God finds her in the wilderness each time—God finds her in the place where she is most vulnerable and where her life hinges on whether she can get the resources needed for survival. Hers is a story about survival of domestic violence and inhospitality in Abraham and Sarah's home and of survival in the wilderness, where food, water, and shelter were in short supply.

In womanist thought and theology, Hagar's story is one of survival. While God is often portrayed as liberator, One who frees persons from various forms of oppression, in this story, God is more concerned with keeping Hagar and her son alive. Hagar is not freed from her oppression at the hands of Sarah. Instead, God hears Hagar and sends her back where she has food and shelter and where she can deliver her baby. Instead of freeing her from the abuse, God makes sure she delivers a healthy baby. Hagar has to return to Sarah and wait—wait to see if she's received back into the household and on what terms; wait to see if the abuse continues; wait to see if her baby is healthy; wait to see if God will keep God's promises to her. She has to play the waiting game to see what will happen. She waits to see if things will turn out as God promises.

Womanists insist that we must expand our understanding of God. Yes, God is about liberation and justice; but God is also about mercy and grace—the things that Hagar needs to receive God's promises. She has enough faith to trust God. Hagar recognizes a dimension of God: the One who sees also hears. The One who hears also makes promises. The One who makes promises is also faithful. Hagar has an independent relationship with God based on her knowledge of God and her personal encounters with the deity. We are asked by womanists to move beyond the liberation paradigm. God not only liberates, but God also provides, nourishes, and insures a future. Hagar's story is a model for a wider understanding of what God is up to in the world.

Hagar's story is also a reminder that God celebrates diversity. She is Egyptian and her son is of mixed parentage and heritage. Millions of Muslims, the majority of whom now live outside the Middle East, claim Abraham as the founding ancestor of Islam. As descendents of Ishmael, Muslims also claim covenant with the God of Abraham. Because of Abraham, Jews, Christians, and Muslims claim a God who hears, sees, makes and keeps promises, and seeks order, beauty, harmony, and unity. But we often behave as if these three great faith traditions have no connection.

In the Bible, the Apostle Paul teaches about Sarah and Hagar in Galatians 4:21–31. He affirms that in God's realm there is diversity: Hagar symbolizes those who obtain God's promise through slavery and law; Sarah symbolizes those who enter God's realm through freedom. Jews,

Christians, and Muslims, belonging to the family of God's promise, are connected.

What else can we say about Hagar? She is a strong woman who is at the mercy of a passive man. Abraham does not stand up for her and provides no protection for her against Sarah's abuse. He seems to go along to get along and does not resist using her as a baby machine. He uses her slave status as justification for having his way with her. He shows no remorse for Hagar's rape and subsequent pregnancy. He heeds Sarah's voice and does not stop Hagar from running away. He does not fight to keep her and his son in the household.

Hagar is in a power struggle with Sarah, the proper mistress of the Abrahamic household. Sarah certainly holds the upper hand over Hagar, yet Hagar manages to survive despite Sarah's efforts to destroy her. Sarah operates out of a sense of her own self-interest and does not care about Hagar beyond how she can be used. Sarah is cold and has no pangs about abusing and sending Hagar away—Sarah, the mother of the faith, is heartless in her dealings with Hagar and expresses no remorse or guilt about her actions. Sarah recognizes her power over Hagar and uses it to her own advantage. When Hagar is no longer useful, Sarah does not hesitate to demand her removal from the home. In this power struggle, Sarah is the winner.

The situation between Sarah and Hagar is reflective of contemporary interactions between some white women and women of color. The history of U.S. slavery is replete with testimonies by black women about how they were treated by their white mistresses. Black women were instrumental in raising white children and keeping white households running; yet black women were raped by the husbands of their mistresses, disrespected by their white charges, and lynched along with black men and children. The Jim Crow era did little to improve the plight of black women, who served as domestics for low wages and no benefits. In addition, it was cadres of white mothers who protested most vociferously against the integration of public schools. I can never forget the images of white mothers yelling racial epithets and spitting on black children as they disembarked from school buses to enter all-white schools. These women mirror too closely Sarah's treatment of Hagar and her child.

Hagar's story is the story of many women whose lives are formed and determined by patriarchal policies and systems. They must deal with issues of homelessness, physical and emotional abuse, women's oppression of other women, survival, empowerment, God's place and role, distrust among women, competition for men's attention and resources. Women have many points of connection across the barriers constructed to keep us separated. It is time for women to be more intentional about building coalitions and taking political actions that benefit all women and do not privilege a small minority at the cost of the majority.

It is important to note that women—white and of color—find ways to overcome the history of oppression and duplicity to forge lasting, meaningful, and authentic relationships. A growing number of white women are acknowledging the misuse of their power and privilege and are making concerted efforts to dismantle their racism and prejudice. Women of color are finding spaces to share their stories with each other to overcome the stereotypes and prejudices within their own communities and across communities of color. It is a testimony to how difficult it is to build cross-cultural relationships that the specter of race and economic superiority still operates in places around the globe. Hagar, our sister, deals with issues of ethnicity, race, and class as well as the demoralizing patriarchal attitudes towards women in general, and foreign women and slave women in particular.

Hagar's story does not just end with the biblical text. Her story has implications for today on many levels. There are many women who wish to be mothers yet find themselves childless. These women experience frustration, heartbreak, and guilt as they try to conceive and are unable to do so. While we have made great strides in the arena of fertility, many women continue to suffer.

Women who are mothers also find themselves in precarious situations—some are trapped in unskilled, low-paying jobs with no adequate and affordable housing, child daycare, or health insurance. They struggle to keep their children safe and long for a better life for them. Some are incarcerated and unable to be mothers to their children. Female inmates are raped and denied access to education and job training. Others succumb to the numbing effects of drugs and are physically and psychologically unable to provide and care for their children. Still others are trapped in unhappy and abusive relationships and marriages. They are so broken and damaged that they have no idea how to be caring and loving mothers. Even women who have material wealth are often torn as they try to balance home and career.

In other words, women have a difficult time in the world. We all have some points of commonality that should lead to coalitions dedicated to improving women's lot around the world. The details will be different, but women have to deal with political, social, cultural, and religious issues that keep us confined. Yet there is strength in numbers. We who are privileged, in whatever ways that might be, must find ways to work in solidarity with sisters across the globe whose resources are limited. We must work diligently to overcome the barriers that patriarchal societies construct to keep people divided and at odds with each other.

Hagar is asked a series of questions: Where have you come from? Where are you going? What troubles you? These are questions women everywhere and under every circumstance must ask each other and themselves.

REFLECTION QUESTIONS

1. In one instance, Hagar runs into the wilderness; in another, she is exiled to it. What do you offer as alternative strategies for Hagar?

2. Have you ever had a wilderness experience? Describe it and explain how you managed to find your way out of it.

3. What is your opinion about why God sends Hagar back to Sarah and into a situation of hardship and abuse? Hagar is focused on the past and God is focused on the future. What future does God envision for Hagar?

4. Who symbolizes the "Hagars"—outcasts, refugees, forgotten, despised, disappeared, expendable—of today? What should our response be to them?

5. What kinds of conversations do you imagine Hagar and Ishmael had about Abraham, Sarah, and Isaac?

6. What systemic issues do you face as a woman? How do you cope with these issues? What can you do to affect policies that relate to the well-being of women?

7. Hagar's story takes place in a context that pits women against each other. What is your experience of conflict with women? What can be done to overcome the barriers that separate women, such as jealousy, envy, competition for men's attention, etc.?

8. What is your personal situation with women who are of a different race than yourself? How are you dealing with the situation?

9. What is your personal situation with women who are of a different class (economic and educational) than yourself? How are you dealing with the situation?

10. What images of women and mothers do you find in the media? Are these images accurate? Explain your answer.

2

SHIPHRAH AND PUAH
What Do We Know about Birthing Babies?

READ

Exodus 1:8–22

FOCUS TEXT

But the midwives feared God; they did not do as the king of Egypt commanded them, but they let the boys live. (Exod. 1:17)

"Did you hear what Pharaoh has planned for those poor little Hebrew boys? You know we can't support that—but what can we do?" The book of Exodus tells how God liberates a group of marginalized people from slavery in Egypt. Known first as the Hebrews and later as Israelites, this group of people is in no position to free themselves. They have a memory of past experiences with a deity who makes promises of progeny and prosperity to their ancestors. The Exodus is about God's grace and presence in human history. In the Hagar story, we discover a God who hears and sees and provides. In

Exodus, God hears the cries of the oppressed Hebrews, sees their condition of servitude, but also liberates them from bondage into freedom and community.

The story of the Exodus begins with the subversive actions of midwives. There is the poignant and comic scene in the classic movie *Gone With the Wind*: Prissy (played by actress Butterfly McQueen), says to Scarlett O'Hara (Vivien Leigh) when they are forced to help Melanie Hamilton (Olivia de Havilland) deliver her baby, "I don't know nothin' 'bout birthin' babies!" The women are called upon to do something of which they have no knowledge. This, however, is not the case with Shiphrah and Puah. The story of the midwives is embedded in the Moses story. There would be no Moses without the ingenuity and defiance of these two courageous women.

The book of Exodus opens with a remembrance of Israel's ancestors. Things have gone well for them in Egypt—they have multiplied and been fruitful, just as God commanded in Genesis 1:28a. Despite the various situations that threatened to abort God's promise to Abraham, the people have prevailed and are living quite well in Egypt. Tension enters the story when we learn that a "new" king takes over Egypt who doesn't know about Joseph or Joseph's family. His lack of memory comes on the heels of the biblical narrator's remembering. The king's ignorance of Joseph's people means that he is not obligated to treat them any differently than the other marginalized and enslaved groups in Egypt. Somehow the story of the Israelites has been lost and they are seen as just another group within the general populace. For a while, the Hebrews seem innocent enough as they provide free labor for the kingdom—they are slaves. But soon, they stand out enough for the new king to recognize them and to feel threatened by them.

The people continue to increase in numbers, and that grabs the king's attention. He is shrewd in his observations and decides that something must be done. What has been a blessing to the Israelites, increased population, is seen as a threat by the king. Ironically, he is the first to express a concern that they may band together, join Egypt's enemies, and leave Egypt. His insight foreshadows the exodus to come later. The new king makes the people work extra hard. Perhaps he thinks exhaustion will slow the population growth of the slaves. He commands his people to "deal shrewdly" with the Israelites and places taskmasters over them to "oppress them with hard labor." The king's first strategy is to enforce labor through excessively abusive methods. The people are forced to build storehouses in Pithom and Rameses—and they do. And they continue producing babies. There are great tensions in the text: between Egyptians and Israelites, slave owners and slaves, the powerful and the powerless. The Israelites are brutalized but they continue to multiply and spread despite the king's effort.

Not to be outdone by a group of lowly slaves, the king tries another tactic—he commands midwives to kill Israelite male babies as soon as they are born. Notice the shift from "Israelite" to "Hebrews" in identifying the slaves. Scholars suggest that the term Hebrews is generic and refers to groups that are marginalized because they have no land or sociopolitical status or power. Such miscellaneous groups are often feared and looked upon with contempt. They simply don't belong except in positions of servitude and bondage.

The king foolishly thinks destroying the males will slow down the population spurt. But again, he is wrong. Two midwives in particular, Shiphrah and Puah, defy the king's order and do not kill the baby boys. Furious over this new turn of events, he summons the two midwives to stand before him and give account of their actions.

The two women stand accused and guilty before the king, but they have a ready defense. They point out the difference between Egyptian and Hebrew women: the Hebrew women are so vigorous that they give birth before the midwife can get to them. It is not clear from the text whether these women are Egyptian midwives assigned to assist the Hebrew women or if they are Hebrew women who have the special skills of midwifery. At any rate, even when the midwives arrive after the babies are born, they refuse to kill the male babies.

They stand tall and give the king their story—and they stick to it. The king does not question them or their actions. Still, he is not to be outdone and issues an edict to all the people of Egypt to kill all Hebrew males under the age of two by tossing them into the Nile River. The king moves from the sublime to the ridiculous in his attempts to stem the tide of the growing Hebrew population. None of his strategies are working and he looks increasingly foolish in his actions. The state-sanctioned genocide fails, leaving the king frustrated and livid. Notice, too, that in the text the king remains unnamed despite his power and authority. The seemingly lowly women, though, have voice and agency, much to the chagrin of the king, no doubt.

Of course, we know something the king does not—God is operating behind the scenes to protect the Israelites. In fact, the two midwives fear the God of Abraham, Isaac, and Jacob and would rather answer to YHWH than to the king of Egypt. This particular group of slaves remembers God's promises to their ancestors. The hope that God's promises will be fulfilled probably prompts them to cry out in their oppression. God chooses to liberate them because of the covenant God made with Abraham. The king commands the midwives to do something that goes against their nature. He tells them to kill when their focus is only on life. The king believes his terrorist edicts will eliminate the population threat; but none of his strategies are effective. The power of life is stronger than that of death. Echoes of Joseph's words to his brothers at the close of Genesis haunt us:

Even though you intended to do harm to me, God intended it for good, in order to preserve a numerous people, as [God] is doing today. (Gen. 50:20)

For their act of defiance against Egypt's monarch, Shiphrah and Puah are rewarded with strong families of their own. The Hebrew population continues to grow. The king has learned nothing from his failures. He is left looking inept because he can do nothing to help his own cause. The story suddenly shifts from the king of Egypt to a small group of women: a woman married to a man from the house of Levi who has just given birth to a son, a sister who watches over this newborn brother, who is hidden in a basket on the Nile River—floating rather than tossed—and a king's daughter who defies her father's edict and rescues the baby boy and adopts him into the royal family.

Moses's story begins with the defiant action of the two midwives against the orders of an anxious, insecure, and desperate king. In most cultures, women deliver their children at home with the help of other women, usually midwives. Midwives are trained to assist in childbirth—they know when the mother should push, how to position the mother just right, where and when the umbilical cord is to be cut, and what to do in cases of emergencies. Midwives are important members of the community who help bring life into the village and world. Midwives, then, assist in the creation process. Whenever we read about births in the Bible, we must assume the presence of a midwife somewhere nearby.

In this text, the midwives have Semitic names but we are not sure if they are Hebrew or Egyptian women. Not only are they named, a rarity in the Bible, but also they have voice and agency. They make a decision not to kill the baby boys and they defend themselves before the king. Articulately testifying on their own behalf, the women demonstrate remarkable courage and cleverness.

Whether Egyptian or Hebrew, the midwives know about Israel's God and they fear this deity. As used here, fear does not mean merely being afraid; it means to hold in reverence and awe—they know this God is much more powerful than the king, who is considered to be a deity too. The Egyptian king is to be worshipped and utterly obeyed. But the midwives recognize a higher power. How they know this, we cannot tell from the text. What we know, for sure, is that they would rather face the wrath of the king than the wrath of God. They are among the God-fearing midwives who defied the king in order to serve God. Their knowledge is sure and they are rewarded for their loyalty and obedience to God.

The king's state policies against the Israelites fail—it is not to be missed that he seeks the lives of the males when the women are the ones undermining his strategies. Not only that, but his own daughter adopts one of the dreaded Hebrews and raises him in the royal palace. The king might have fared better to exterminate the girls.

The midwives continue with their work and go on to raise families without any interference from the king. Perhaps he dismisses them as crazy women; he certainly does not ask any questions about the childbirth process. Nor does he punish them for their acts of defiance. We may assume the women also taught other women midwiving skills, since there is always a need for midwives.

In this text, the midwives are subversive and reverse the course of action laid out by the king. These two midwives, who may have been singled out because they are leaders of the "National Midwife Society," find a way to speak truth to power: life triumphs over death despite, or in spite of, the state's power and resources. For those doing the king's work, there is no need for questions or critique. The Hebrew babies are seen as collateral damage in maintaining the state's security interests. The midwives, though, hold a different vision of community—one that celebrates life rather than one that deals death. They bring life out of a death command and create a space for the future of the Israelites and, by extension, for all marginalized people who are brutalized, neglected, and exterminated.

Instead of killing off the baby boys, they let them live. In a patriarchal society that values males, it is a wonder that the king wanted the girls to live. In this reversal, the midwives create their own reversal—both the girls and the boys live. Of course, the question must be raised—just how many male babies actually died as a result of the king's actions? We can only assume that many died, even though the text does not indicate the plight of the other baby boys. We hope that some males survived, but how many and what manner, we cannot say for certain. The text is not as interested in answering our questions as it is in highlighting the miraculous survival of at least one male child, Moses.

Whatever the number of boys rescued, Shiphrah and Puah take great risks to resist the systemic attempts of the king. By their example, they show how the actions of the powerless can affect the efficacy of state policies. Their quiet defiance makes a way for life to survive. They give hope to all who feel the oppressive burden of state-sanctioned programs that lead to death: the expansion of the prison industrial complex, inadequate or nonexistent health care, limited social services, cutbacks in education in favor of more money for military defense, lack of affordable housing and childcare—the list is endless. But we are not to lose hope in the struggle for justice and peace. By remembering the story of these two midwives, we remember that humankind has some power, but God has all power—power, even, to bring life out of death.

REFLECTION QUESTIONS

1. More women in the United States are opting for home births. How have the roles of the midwife changed as technology has become more advanced?

2. What have been your experience(s) of childbirth? What value do you think there is in home births with the assistance of a midwife or doula?

3. If midwife is a metaphor for the birth of something new, what new possibility are you midwiving in your life, in your church, in your community?

4. Why do you think the king keeps insisting on programs to kill Hebrew boys? Why didn't he think of something else to do?

5. In what ways are societal structures and systems still trying to kill off male babies and young men?

6. A midwife, Ms. Mary McGraw, delivered me. Until my early teens, whenever I saw her, she always remembered my name and birthday. What kind of relationships do doctors of obstetrics and genecology have with the mothers and the babies they deliver today?

7. In what ways are you like Shiphrah and Puah? In what ways are you different?

8. What current local, national, and federal programs undermine life and survival?

9. What can you do to address policies that do not support the well-being of persons and communities?

10. In what ways is God *still* bringing life out of death?

3

MIRIAM

Am I My Brother's Keeper?

READ

Exodus 2:1–10, 15:20–21
Numbers 12:1–6

FOCUS TEXT

Then the prophet Miriam, Aaron's sister, took a tambourine in her hand; and all the women went out after her with tambourines and with dancing. And Miriam sang to them:

"Sing to [YHWH], for [YHWH] has triumphed gloriously;
horse and rider [YHWH] has thrown into the sea."
(Exod. 15:20–21)

"Look at me! Hear me! Love me! I'm not talking to men—I'm talking to God." The Exodus story that begins with ancestral memory and moves to conflict with a new Egyptian king now suddenly shifts to a domestic scene. At the end of the first chapter of the book of Exodus, we are left with the king's dastardly and murderous edict to drown baby boys:

Then Pharaoh commanded all his people, "Every boy
that is born to the Hebrews you shall throw into the
Nile, but you shall let every girl live." (Exod. 1:22)

The Nile River, a source of life for major parts of Africa,
is now a resting place for the dead, holding the tender bones
of baby boys drowned for no reason other than their gender
and ethnicity.

The king declares the Hebrews nobodies, of no value,
and only to be controlled and contained. Yet, in the midst of
the king's intent to deal only hard labor and death, we read
in Exodus 2 that a man and woman, both of priestly lineages,
marry. To make matters even more interesting, the woman
gives birth to a son. In the realm of Egypt's state of terror
against the Hebrews, life keeps rolling on—there are wed-
dings and births even though the Hebrews are Egypt's declared public enemy number one. So we are on edge to find
out what happens to this baby boy whose fate is to be
drowned in the Nile. The mother, however, sees her "fine"
baby and hides him. The word translated "fine" is the same
Hebrew word (tôb) that God uses to describe aspects of
creation—good (see Gen. 1:31). We suspect, then, that this
particular baby boy is not just any precious baby boy.

Like the midwives, Shiphrah and Puah, this unnamed
mother saves her son—she cannot kill the life she has
birthed. We wonder how many other mothers hide their off-
spring in order to save them from death. When she can no
longer conceal his presence, she carefully packages him and
places him among the reeds (sŭp) at the edge of the Nile
River, foreshadowing the name of the waters through which
the Hebrew slaves will navigate to freedom later. The child
floats at the edge of the waters of liberation.

His older sister keeps vigil at a distance to see what happens—will he die or somehow live? We next see the king's
daughter, bathing in the Nile, the very place of death for the

Hebrews. Despite the edict to toss baby boys into the river, Pharaoh's daughter bathes there. We are not to miss the paradox of this situation—the river is a tomb for some and a place of refreshment for others. We cannot know just how many bones are interred on the floor of the river—how many sons, brothers, nephews, and grandsons make the river bed their final resting place. Pharaoh's daughter sees a basket and hears the cries of an infant; her actions here mirror those of God towards Hagar in Genesis 16 and 21.

The Egyptian princess immediately recognizes the infant as one of the Hebrews; she doesn't question how he survived or how he came to be floating in a watertight basket on the Nile. She does not kill him nor does she order her attendants to do so. The order of the day, issued by her very father, is again subverted. Instead, she takes pity on the infant—the Hebrew word *hāmal* carries the meaning of "compassion." She is moved to compassion and action, in stark contrast to her father; she becomes the infant's savior and protects him— all in defiance of her father's royal policy. Again, women, including his own daughter, are undermining the king.

The unnamed sister of the infant emerges from the shadows with a plan. She speaks and acts as if the princess has no choice but to keep the child alive and safe. What a nervy young woman she is, a Hebrew and a slave, to approach the princess of Egypt. The sister fetches her mother who is hired by the princess to nurse the baby.

What a turn of events. We are more than surprised and now deeply suspect that this manchild is no ordinary boy. We suspect that there will be great things in store for him. His mother, surrounded by his father and siblings, nurtures the child. He is turned over to the Egyptian princess when he is weaned; she names him Moses and stakes full claim to the child. This episode provides a rare picture of women working together across racial, ethnic, and class lines. The enslaved are treated fairly, the free woman has compassion, and the infant boy is saved. The women talk to each other, share ideas, and cooperate in order to save the child. This story stands in stark contrast to that of Sarah and Hagar.

The king, who wants Hebrew boys drowned, now harbors one in his palace and must acknowledge him as his grandson. Do you think the king's plan has utterly failed?

In this text, we are introduced to Moses's sister, Miriam. Her story is embedded in the Moses corpus. When we meet her, she is the nameless sister of a male infant saved from the Egyptian king's murderous edict. She reappears in Exodus 15 with a name and mission. She is Miriam the prophet. She has a share in Moses's ministry and in the liberation of the Hebrews. What's more, she is a songwriter-poet, dancer, and leader. It is she who leads the women in a celebratory song and dance of liberation at the edge of the reeds.

Commonly known as the "Song of Miriam," Exodus 15:21 is believed to be the oldest poem in the Bible and likely composed near the time of the actual exodus experience. We ought not be surprised to see Miriam in a leadership role—her initiative during Moses's infancy foreshadows a woman who takes charge in creative ways, even in the face of danger and distress. We expect her to be held in high regard among the people. Her song imparts hope and inspiration to women and to men who are on the verge of new life and new hope.

The prophet Micah affirms Miriam's importance and her contribution to the community during the Exodus and wilderness sojourn:

> For I [God] brought you up from the land of Egypt,
>   and redeemed you from the house of slavery;
> and I sent before you Moses, Aaron, and Miriam.
>
> (Micah 6:4)

Miriam, the prophet and spokesperson for and to God, comes from priestly roots—both her father and mother are of priestly lineage. She leads the women (and probably men, too) in song, dance, and prayer. While we do not know what precise role she played in the liberation of her people, we are left with a picture of a powerful woman—one who is a creative presence. Her nervy approach to the princess of Egypt shows she has no shame and doesn't mind taking the initiative. We can imagine her encouraging her people toward freedom. Perhaps some were skeptical about Moses's capacity to effect their freedom; Miriam may have spoken up for her brother. Surely she supported his leadership, and we wonder what tasks he may have asked her to perform. Perhaps she was the one who always had a word of cheer and a prayer for endurance—the work didn't stop while Moses and Aaron appealed to the king of Egypt. Someone had to keep the people's spirit strong, and Miriam may have been that one. Through her songs and prayers, Miriam may have encouraged the people to dream about freedom and to hold on until their change came. It may have been Miriam who kept the flame and hope of freedom strong among her demoralized people. If she did nothing more than these things, she is worthy to be remembered and revered. In every age and time, we need people who will inspire others and kept them focused on a goal. We need people who never waver in their determination to achieve a dream—Miriam was that person for the Israelites.

As we have seen with other leaders, the text does not describe Miriam as perfect. Of course, perfection is not a criterion for strong and effective leadership. Miriam is a courageous, vital, creative woman. And we know that such women don't linger long in the biblical text; we are not surprised, then, when Miriam is put in her place. A defining moment in Miriam's story occurs in Numbers 12. Here, she and her brother Aaron are gossiping and complaining about Moses. They seem to be caught up in a fairly typical web of sibling rivalry. Moses gets more attention, even though both Miriam and Aaron have been instrumental in the Hebrew liberation movement. They present two issues that on the surface seem unrelated: Moses's marriage to a Cushite woman and Moses's growing leadership and authority.

The presenting issue is Moses's marriage to a foreigner. Such marriages will be taboo later in Israel's history; but here, the great liberator, Moses, is married to a foreign woman. Reference to Moses's Cushite wife is found only here in Numbers 12. She is nameless and never speaks, but her appearance raises a number of questions: is she the same woman elsewhere named Zipporah, Moses's Midianite wife? Is she a second wife Moses has taken? If so, what happened to Zipporah? Does Moses have a thing for foreign women? Is there something about this particular woman, other than her nationality or ethnicity, that irks Miriam and Aaron? Cush, or Ethiopia, is identified with wealth and privilege; does this Cushite woman display an attitude of arrogance or prejudice or class discrimination? Once again, we are confronted with a number of questions and few answers.

The text reveals more about the domestic situation of Moses with Zipporah from Midian than of the Cushite woman, referred to only here in Numbers. Cush refers to a region south of Egypt, ancient Nubia and modern Ethiopia. Biblical references characterize the region as wealthy and inhabited by strong warriors. Moses's marriage to a Cushite woman is seen as problematic for Miriam and Aaron (or, at least, for the biblical narrator) because such intercultural marriages are prohibited later (see Deut. 7:3, Num. 25, and Ezra 9–10). The liberator and prophet of God violates the rules against intermarriages with foreign women—but Moses, as we have seen, is a different kind of leader. In this Numbers text, his marriage is condoned by God and implies that the Hebrews, from early in their history, was a mixed group of people; thus, our understandings of the Israelites must include a wide range of ethnicities and nationalities under one God. Moses is a different kind of leader and is given sanction and approval by God, despite the appearances to others, namely Miriam and Aaron. The Cushite wife is mentioned and she disappears. The issue shifts to leadership concerns.

The second complaint that Miriam and Aaron have against Moses exposes feelings about their own leadership in the post-exodus community. Both have been instrumental in the Hebrew liberation movement—Aaron standing with Moses before Pharaoh and Miriam composing and choreographing liberation songs and dances. Miriam and Aaron sullenly ask, "What about us?" They question the legitimacy of their own prophetic gifts, which are overshadowed by Moses's. In Numbers 11, Moses expresses to Joshua a desire that all of God's people had the gift of prophecy:

> But Moses said to [Joshua] "Are you jealous for my sake? Would that all [YHWH]'s people were prophets, and that [YHWH] would put [YHWH]'s spirit on them!" (Num. 11:29)

On the heels of Moses's wish, we find Miriam and Aaron grumbling about Moses's leadership. It is not clear why, of all the people in the camp, it is Miriam and Aaron who question Moses's leadership. Miriam's prophetic leadership is not questioned and seems to be a relatively normal occurrence. Both Miriam and Aaron want it known that God also speaks through them and not just through Moses. Both feel slighted, but it is not clear whom they blame—the people or God. What is clearer is that both siblings feel they are equal to Moses. Aaron spoke on Moses's behalf in front of Pharaoh—where is Aaron's due respect and appreciation? Miriam saved Moses from extermination, kept the spirits of the people high, and helped them maintain hope when all hope seemed foolish—where is Miriam's due respect and appreciation? While Moses stammered and hemmed and hawed before God, Aaron gave voice to Moses's thoughts and commitments while Miriam sang and danced in eloquent and celebratory style. In a moment of Miriam and Aaron's hurt feelings, Moses's shortcomings come front and center.

Notice, though, what happens in the text. God calls a conference with Moses, Aaron, and Miriam. It seems that God wants to nip this situation in the bud—the confrontation is about to be on—we can hardly wait to see what happens. Miriam and Aaron seem justified in their feelings; their leadership has taken a backseat to Moses. Perhaps Miriam and Aaron welcomed the conference—finally, they will get their due accolades and affirmation. But they, and we, are surprised when God speaks—God is upset with the pair. It's as though God says to Miriam and Aaron:

"Look, let's be clear. You two are good prophets and leaders and without you my people would not be free. But let there be no mistake about it, Moses is my main man! When I speak to you, I do so through dreams and visions and riddles. But haven't you noticed that I speak to Moses directly, mouth to mouth and in plain language? Don't you think there's a reason for that? I trust Moses and know I can rely on him. Yes, he had doubts and questions. Yes, he wanted someone else to do this work, but when he committed himself, he totally committed. Having seen how I deal with Moses, how dare you speak against him? Here you are in the wilderness, trying to get to the land where I'm leading you, and all you can do is talk about Moses behind his back? Why do you care who his wife is? What they do behind closed tents is their business. If you spent more time taking care of your business and doing the work I've given you, you'd have less time to whine and complain. There is much freedom work left to do and all you can do is backstab and undermine Moses's leadership. Know this, Miriam and Aaron, I'm not having this!"

It is clear that God has a preference for Moses—Moses is different. His authority comes from his personality, his willingness to speak for God, and his capacity to speak for the people. God's remarks are directed to Aaron and Miriam but only Miriam is chastised for her comments. She is afflicted with a skin disease—she becomes leprous and white as snow. Leprosy in the Bible is a generic, unspecified skin condition (see Lev. 13), but is not the same as the modern Hansen's disease. "Leprosy" often results in scaly and pale skin. Aaron is scared when he looks at Miriam and sees she is pale as snow. It is ironic to note that Miriam complains about Moses's dark-skinned wife and now Miriam herself is whitewashed.

It is not clear why Miriam is afflicted but Aaron is not—especially since they are partners in complaining about Moses. Some have suggested that if Aaron were stricken, his status as priest would have been in jeopardy. The people would not accept him as a priest if there were any hint of impurity in him. Again, a woman takes the fall for a man. To his credit, Aaron appeals to Moses to help Miriam lest she become "like one stillborn, whose flesh is half consumed when it comes out of its mother's womb." Her condition resembles a kind of flesh-eating disorder and Aaron intercedes on her behalf with Moses. In addition to his other charismatic gifts, Moses has the power to ask God for her healing. Instead of ignoring Miriam or being vindictive, Moses prays to God for her healing (see Num. 12:13). This is a curious turn of events: early on, Miriam saves Moses. Now Moses saves Miriam—one good turn deserves another.

God seems reluctant to heal her immediately. God seems to punish Miriam for her thoughts and words. God reckons her offense to the shame of a father spitting in the face of a child. Such action expresses contempt (see Deut. 25:9), insult (see Isa. 50:6), or impurity (see Lev. 15:18). God's word about Miriam implies that she is unclean because of her skin condition and because of her thoughts about Moses. The bottom line of God's indictment is that Moses is God's special servant and Miriam has no right to question either God's judgment or Moses's leadership. Miriam's skin condition makes her unclean and she needs to be quarantined from the community for a period of seven days. When her seven days are up, she reunites with the community and the people leave Hazeroth and head to Paran.

God chastises both her and Aaron, but only Miriam is "punished." The people, acknowledging Miriam's leadership and importance to the community, refuse to move on their journey without her (see Num. 12:15b). Although Miriam feels slighted, she learns that the people love and respect her. Note that from the moment she criticizes Moses, Miriam is silent—sufficiently put in her place in the patriarchal narrative, invisible and silent. A woman who emerged from the shadows by the Nile to make sure her brother was safe now simply disappears. A woman who sang and danced is silenced and her feet stopped. She is absent from the remainder of the narrative until we learn of her death. She was buried at Kadesh, in the wilderness of Zin. Her final resting place is a place that lacks water. Ironically, her best moments occurred near water—the Nile River where she oversaw the rescue of Moses and on the banks of the Sea of Reeds (Red Sea) when she celebrated the freedom of her people. Neither she nor Moses, however, reach the promised land. And for her attempt to have her gifts recognized, she was laid to rest in a dry and arid place.

Miriam is certainly a "bad girl" even though we don't have a full portrait of her. The only men she is attached to in the text are Moses and Aaron, her brothers. We conclude that she never marries nor does she have children. Hers is a life devoted to others: saving her brother Moses and saving her people. Miriam is a "career" woman whose work is done in public and political spheres. She is not described physically, so we don't know if she is beautiful, tall, lean, or any physical characteristics. She is stricken with leprosy, which often brings deforming consequences. Despite the lack of a full picture of her, Miriam displays resourcefulness and courage, takes the initiative to keep her brother safe, exercises power and leadership, and expresses her creative and poetic self. At the same time, she seems to resist a change in leadership style and mode. Her charismatic gifts of prophecy, song, poetry, and dance are piled in with the gifts of others and become less prominent than in days past. In the Bible, she shifts from being an inspiring, upbeat, prophetic, and charismatic leader into a gossipy, complaining, bitter woman. She shifts from being a confident, feisty woman to one who is insecure and envious. She moves from nameless presence to one who has a name, agency, voice, and title. As with other bad girls, she is hailed as an individual, powerful personality but is put in her place—one of silence and powerlessness.

REFLECTION QUESTIONS

1. How can women claim their power, leadership, and authority? From where do you think Miriam's courage and power come? From where does your power and courage come?

2. What do you think Miriam's message was? To whom were her messages addressed?

3. In what ways is charismatic leadership expressed today? How does charismatic leadership differ from celebrity or personality-driven leadership?

4. What are Miriam's leadership strengths and weaknesses? In what ways are you like Miriam? How are you different? How do you deal with anxiety and/or insecurity?

5. What does her song in Exodus 15 say to the Israelites? What values does she highlight?

6. Early in her life, Miriam demonstrates her capacity to work with other women, including the powerful princess of Egypt. Why do you think Miriam had issues with Moses's Cushite wife?

7. Moses's marriage to a foreign woman demonstrates the diversity of the Israelite community. How does his domestic situation speak to how we should understand community?

8. Do you ever feel that your gifts and contributions to church and society are undervalued and unrecognized? How do you handle those feelings?

9. Has your leadership ever been challenged? On what grounds has the critique been focused? How did you handle the challenge to your leadership?

10. What advice do you offer women who are talented but frustrated because they have limited outlets for their leadership and creativity?

4

ZIPPORAH
What Won't I Do For My Man?

READ

Exodus 4:18–26, 18:1–7

FOCUS TEXT

But Zipporah took a flint and cut off her son's foreskin, and touched Moses's feet with it, and said, "Truly you are a bridegroom of blood to me!" (Exod. 4:25)

"I don't know what your God is up to, but I have no choice but to take matters into my own hands!" Zipporah's story is embedded in the Moses narratives. She is one of seven daughters born to Reuel (also known in various texts as Jethro and Hobab), the priest of Midian. Midian is the region Moses flees to after his murder of an Egyptian who killed one of his fellow Hebrew kin. According to the biblical record, Midian is occupied by the descendants of Abraham and Keturah (see Gen. 25:2). While in Midian, Moses re-

ceives his commission from God to return to Egypt to free the Hebrew people.

When we meet Zipporah, she is among a nameless group of sisters drawing water for the family sheep. A group of shepherds chases them from the well and Moses comes to the rescue. He then waters the sheep for the women. The sisters return home much sooner than they should and explain to their father than an "Egyptian" has helped them. The father sends them back to invite the young man to dinner. Moses not only stays for dinner, he takes a job with Jethro and marries one of the priest's daughters. Zipporah and Moses have two sons: Gershom (whose name means "I have been an alien in a foreign land") and Eliezer (whose name means "the God of my father was my help and delivered me from the sword of Pharaoh"). As with most stories in the Bible, we have to ask the pertinent question: about whom is the story focused? Although Zipporah is the subject of this study unit, we quickly recognize that the story is all about Moses. Zipporah helps move his story along just as the midwives, Shiphrah and Puah do, as Miriam and Pharaoh's daughter do—Moses owes his very existence to the quick thinking and courageous acts of women.

Moses, in many ways, symbolizes the sojourn of Israel. He is caught between a rock and a hard place. He should have been killed at birth but he survives. Not only does he survive, he is raised and educated in Pharaoh's palace as the royal grandson. We do not know if Pharaoh had other children or if Moses's adopted mom had other children. Despite the privileges Moses enjoys in Pharaoh's house, his early years with his Hebrew family leaves him identifying with the enslaved Hebrews. He is neither Egyptian nor Hebrew, but rather a blend of both. In dress and manner, he is Egyptian. In his heart and allegiances, he is Hebrew. His name, given by Pharaoh's daughter, highlights his identity crisis—the Egyptian gives him a name derived from a

Hebrew verb meaning "to draw out." Linguistically, his name exposes a duality that is manifested in his dual identity as Egyptian and Hebrew.

As an adult, he continues to live with a sense of "double consciousness," a term used by African American scholar and activist W. E. B. DuBois, to describe the bicultural and conflicting identities that African Americans experience in the United States. By coining this term, DuBois makes it clear that blacks in the United States recognize their African origins although they don't often know specific details about geographical origins, language, culture, religion, and so forth. At the same time, blacks recognize their U.S. citizenship that brings challenges such as slavery, Jim Crow, and ongoing racial, social, economic, and political discrimination and privileges such as opportunities for education and upward mobility. African Americans are torn between being "black" and being "American," two identities often in conflict with each other. Blacks are required to negotiate between these two allegiances—just as Moses struggles to find a place. Moses does not fit into the Egyptian culture nor does he fit in Israelite culture—he is torn. He kills an Egyptian for beating a Hebrew (see Exod. 2:11), implying that his allegiance is to his kin people. The next day, however, he stops a fight between two Hebrews and they rail against him because they do not identify with him (see Exod. 2:13–14). Then, to complicate matters even more, his adopted grandfather seeks to kill him for Moses's murder of the Egyptian. Moses's life moves in curious ways—he is out (a slave), then he's in (adopted into his oppressor's family), and then he's out again (a fugitive from justice on the charge of murder). Will he ever be "in" again? Moses has no place to be somebody, a man without a country or home. Now he is in Midian and clearly an outsider—the sisters identify him as an Egyptian.

In addition to his conundrum about his Egyptian and Hebrew identities, Moses has assimilated into the Midian culture. He marries a woman from Midian and has children with her—he's not merely bicultural, Moses is tricultural. To highlight his identity issue, he names his first son Gershom, the Hebrew word for "alien" and declares through his son's name that he "has been an alien residing in a foreign land" (see Exod. 2:22). Moses is a soul without a home or resting place.

After a back and forth exchange with God, Moses finally agrees to return to Egypt to free his Hebrew kin. His explanation to Jethro is circumspect—he states he wants to go back to Egypt to see how his kinfolk are. Moses does not share his theophany with Jethro but gets the blessing of the priest nevertheless. Moses packs up his wife and two sons and heads back to Egypt. But his challenges are not yet over:

> On the way, at a place where [Moses, Zipporah, and Gershom] spent the night, [YHWH] met him and tried to kill him. (Exod. 4:24)

It seems that Moses is not even "in" with God. We presume that the Moses family is on their way to Egypt; but we have no clue why God wants to kill him. This verse is problematic on a couple of levels: Moses survived the terrorist tactics of the Egyptian king; Moses is the crown prince and potential heir to the Egyptian throne; Moses is exiled as a fugitive from justice; and Moses has been convinced by God to return to Egypt. The God who sees, hears, and liberates seeks Moses to kill him. What is going on in this text? If you are stumped, you are not alone! It has been suggested that the ways of God are so mysterious that it is not possible to explain the desire of God to kill the very one saved and chosen for liberation. This explanation is not satisfactory, however. Others suggest that this text is about the origins of the rite of circumcision—but does not connect with Abraham. But the God who seeks Moses's life is not unlike the God who commands Abraham to kill his heir apparent, Isaac.

There is no explaining this God who gives life and on occasion seeks death from the very ones to whom he promises blessings.

Now, instead of Moses doing the rescuing, Zipporah steps into those shoes. Moses is stricken with a mysterious illness and is on the verge of death. The text says that God is seeking Moses's life. We are not told why and are puzzled by this turn of events. God has gone to great lengths to convince Moses to return to Egypt and set the enslaved Israelites free. Moses finally agrees to return to Egypt and on the way, God suddenly wants him dead. It is not much of a stretch to see parallels with Jacob's journey—see Genesis 28:10–22 and 32:22–32. Instead of wrestling with God, as Jacob does, Moses is a passive victim—until Zipporah takes action.

It is not clear how she knows that God is trying to kill Moses. Does he go into convulsions? Does he foam at the mouth? Does he make choking sounds? Does he grab his chest as if having a heart attack? Does she witness the entrance of some strange intruder who attacks Moses? Does Moses display his anxiety with flailing limbs and strangled cries? Does she see an apparition, a menacing ghost moving towards her son and husband? Does she see a sudden panic in her husband's eyes? The text is strangely silent on the matter.

Despite the lack of details, we see Zipporah acting—she circumcises her son with a flint and touches Moses's genitals ("feet" being an euphemism for genitals in the Bible). There are two probable reasons for her actions. Some scholars believe her act is part of a larger healing ritual grounded in the religious practices of various communities in the ancient Near East. Through her priestly act (later in Israel's history, priests were assigned the job of circumcising the males), Moses recovers and lives to rescue his people. Others suggest she performs a ritual requirement of adolescent males as preparation for marriage and her words echo the closing words of an ancient ritual. Circumcision in ancient Egypt would have been performed on adolescent males rather than on infants.

In ancient Israel, circumcision is symbolic of a man's agreement and faithfulness to the covenant between God and Abraham—see Genesis 17:13. It is not stated in the text whether Moses had been circumcised as an infant; as a Hebrew, he should have undergone the rite when he was eight days old. With a death sentence, however, over the heads of Hebrew newborns and later all boys under two, his parents may have forgone the ritual altogether. Further, scholars suggest that Moses fails to circumcise his own sons; the reasons why are not clear but may be related to the nature of mixed marriages at that time.

What the text reveals is that Zipporah steps between God and Moses by performing a blood ritual. She initiates Moses's rescue, and her actions are efficacious and Moses is saved. Zipporah acts as a priest and savior to and for her husband. She stands against God in her effort to save her man. Not only is Zipporah a woman, she is also a foreign woman. Here, again, we find a reversal of what we would normally expect to see in the biblical text. The quick-witted Zipporah intervenes. In addition to saving his life, she gives him another identity: the bridegroom of blood—hardly what we associate with bridegrooms. We expect them to be happy, not smeared with blood. We expect them to be celebrating, not escaping death. We expect them to be surrounded by joyous relatives and friends, not struggling to survive in the wilderness. In this episode, Zipporah is not just Moses's wife and the mother of his sons—she is also his priest. In this way, she is like her father, Jethro. She performs a priestly act and symbolizes her father, who is Moses's father-in-law, the priest of Midian. Zipporah mirrors the reversal that the women in Moses's world have taken on—she provides the means by which Moses survives. She takes on a male role in order to save her husband. And we know what happens to women who behave as men—they meet some kind of un-timely or brutal demise or silencing. We are not sure what happens to Zipporah, but we can expect her to disappear from the narrative. And, indeed, she does.

God leaves Moses alone and he seems transformed. If we follow the analogy between the stories of Jacob and Moses, then Moses would have been transformed, changed in some way because of Zipporah's actions on his behalf. Jacob was left with a limp from his encounter with God; Moses is left bloody from his encounter with God. Instead of thanking Zipporah and honoring her initiative on his behalf, Moses sends Zipporah and their sons back to live with her father in Midian. It is not clear why or when Moses sends her back. Some suggest he does so to save them from the horrors of his encounters with Pharaoh. But the text does not state that others sent their families away to avoid the rigors of libera-tion works. Others suggest that he does so because he is dis-gusted and angry at her heroic, but male, actions in the cir-cumcision—even though her actions saved his life. Jethro, after some time, takes them back to Moses. By this time, Moses has led the people from Egypt into the wilderness near Mt. Sinai. We have seen that the wilderness is a place of transformation—on the way to Egypt, Moses has a life-changing encounter with God and a life-giving encounter with Zipporah.

Zipporah and Moses seem an unlikely couple—she is a peasant girl and he, though Hebrew, grows up as Egyptian royalty. Although Moses is a fugitive from justice, he lives a fairly normal life—he marries, has children, and is gainfully employed working for his father-in-law. It is likely that Moses learned much priestly knowledge from Jethro as well as about farming and shepherding. It is even more likely that Zipporah also learned some skills of the priest. It has been suggested that her quick action on Moses's behalf stems from her intimate knowledge of priestly work since she grew up in the household of a priest. She would have been privy to various rituals and would have some understandings of the healing arts.

Zipporah is smart, courageous, and has the gift of healing. She is adventurous and brave—she leaves her family and support system to follow her husband to Egypt. They both are willing to risk a dangerous situation and she does not resist. Despite her initiative, though, her status as a woman means that she is not in full control of her life: her father gives her away in marriage; her husband sends her back to her father; her father takes her back to her husband—she must have-felt like a ping pong ball between the two men. And we have no idea how she feels about being shuttled back and forth. What we know of her is that she is enterprising, quick to act, and loyal to her husband. When her husband's life is on the line, she springs into action. Her bloody ritual saves her husband and possibly her sons. No mere passive and compliant woman, Zipporah is resourceful and bodacious—she stands up to God, who has a death grip on Moses, and she changes the outcome of the encounter. With bloody hands and pounding heart, Zipporah is empowered to bring life out of the grips of death. Still, she loses her voice and disappears from the narrative—like the midwives, and like Moses's birth and adoptive mothers.

REFLECTION QUESTIONS

1. Moses has a history of being rescued by women. How does Zipporah's act differ from Miriam's?
2. What are some issues faced by intercultural, interfaith, and interracial couples? How can the church support them?

3. What advice do you offer Zipporah about her father's role in her marriage?

4. Zipporah leaves the comforts of her home to follow Moses to Egypt. Why do you think he sends her back to her father? Do you think he divorces her? If so, why would he do that?

5. How do you imagine the Israelites felt when Jethro shows up with Moses's wife and two sons?

6. How can the church truly be a welcoming place for all people?

7. Have you ever left the comforts of home for a new place? Why did you leave? What resources helped you to settle into your new location?

8. How do you deal with loneliness and feelings of isolation and alienation?

9. How do you think Moses reacts after Zipporah circumcises their son and saves his life?

10. Why do you believe the biblical writers dismiss the women responsible for keeping Moses alive?

5

BATHSHEBA
Until You Do Right By Me . . .

READ

2 Samuel 11:1–26, 12:24–25
1 Kings 1:11–32

FOCUS TEXT

The woman conceived; and she sent and told David,
"I am pregnant." (2 Sam. 11:5)

"What did I do to deserve all this misery? And David—he's not all that!" Her name epitomes the quintessential bad girl . . . Bathsheba. She is accused of causing David's troubles in his personal life. Modern interpretations of her story have symbolized her as the dangerous other—the woman who seduces good men into evil deeds. Her story, however, has been oversimplified and distorted so that David becomes a hero despite his actions against her and her husband, Uriah. When her son Solomon becomes king, we find out that she

is no mere one-dimensional sex object; rather, she is a complex, layered personality who grows into a woman of agency and voice. Although her story is part of the Davidic corpus, she plays a major role in securing the throne for Solomon and continues to play a major role as queen mother.

Bathsheba is the daughter of Eliam, the son of Ahitophel, an advisor to David. She is married to Uriah, a Hittite member of David's army. It is likely that her family is of non-Israelite origins; it is speculated that part of her name, "Sheba," is a reference to a foreign god. We learn right away that Bathsheba is confined by the limitations of patriarchy because her identity is wrapped up in whose daughter and wife she is. She is not an independent woman who is making her own way in the world. She is a daughter and wife of powerful men, men who are connected to David—her father is one of David's advisors and her husband is one of David's ablest soldiers. She is a woman of importance to the Davidic court, yet he is willing to violate the trust of his advisor and soldier to satisfy his lust. A seemingly innocent remark is made about her: "the woman was very beautiful" (2 Sam. 11:2b). This remark implies that David cannot help wanting her—that it is her fault that David strays, that David (and any man) is helpless before the beauty of a woman. Her identity, apart from the men in her life, is also wrapped up in her body and her beauty. Shame on her for being pretty and irresistible.

David sends his army, under the able leadership of Joab, to fight the Ammonites at Rabbah (east of the Jordan River), while he stays home. The text does not tell us why David is not out fighting, especially since this was "the time of the year when kings go out to battle." His troops are on the battlefield, but David remains in Jerusalem. Since we know David to be a strong warrior (see my chapters on David in *Misbehavin' Monarchs: Exploring Biblical Rulers of Questionable Virtue*, chapters 3 and 4), we are alerted that something unusual is about to happen.

David sees Bathsheba, inquires about who she is, and learns that she is the wife of one of his outstanding soldiers. Armed with this important information, David sends for her and commits adultery. The most powerful man in the land makes a decision to have sex with another man's wife—we know that David can be ruthless on the battlefield, but this act of lust and power does not fit one who is considered the apple of God's eye. It is not clear from the text what actually happens behind the closed doors of the royal chambers. Some speculate that Bathsheba seduces David—that she knows the king is home and is likely to walk out on his terrace to see her bathing, that she times her bath in order to give the monarch a show. Her motivation, it is suggested, is based on the fact that she has not had children with Uriah. If she can become pregnant by David, her son could become king. There are a lot of assumptions in this reasoning that are difficult to reconcile. There are too many what-ifs for this to be a reasonable plan. It seems unlikely that Bathsheba hatches a plan to entrap David; and even if she did, we know David to be much more savvy than to fall for such a plan. We don't know if she deliberately seduces David or not. What we do know is that when the king sends for her, she has no choice but to go.

We know that David initiates contact with her, even after he learns that she is a married woman. We don't know if she tries to resist David's advances; her resistance probably would have been ineffective because David has made up his mind that she will be his, at least for those amorous moments. After sexual intercourse, he sends her away. There is no indication in the text that he even gives her or his actions a second thought. His lust is satisfied and life goes on as usual. That is, until he receives a note from her announcing her pregnancy.

We are told in the text that she was bathing as part of a cleansing ritual signaling the end of her menstrual period. With her husband being away at war, there is no doubt that the child is David's (see 2 Sam. 11:4b). Whether she seduces David or not, he is responsible for his actions. He is willing to jeopardize his crown for a moment of lust. He plays the peeping Tom and uses his royal prerogative and power to have his way with another man's wife. It doesn't matter that David already has a number of wives and concubines—he exercises no discretion and insists on having his way. David seems unconcerned about his one-night stand—other than satisfying his libido, there is nothing else Bathsheba can offer David. He gains nothing politically by developing a relationship with her; she is convenient, and the deed is done. But now, everything has changed. Words that often bring joy and expectation—"I'm pregnant"—now bring dread and a need for a cover-up. And David goes to great lengths to cover up his deed.

His first solution is to send for Uriah. Commander-in-Chief Joab releases Uriah from duty and sends him to Jerusalem. Joab does not question why David wants to see Uriah; he simply follows David's orders. Uriah arrives and stands before David. David feigns interest in the war and without explanation sends Uriah home to "wash his feet," which is an euphemism for sexual intercourse. David reasons that if Uriah sleeps with his wife, both he and Bathsheba can pretend that the baby is Uriah's. A great plan that fails—Uriah, loyal soldier, refuses to enjoy the comforts of home when others are toughing it out in the war zone. Instead, Uriah sleeps among the other servants of David.

David's second solution is to get Uriah drunk, hoping that in an intoxicated state, Uriah will be tempted to have sex with his wife. But David's plan is foiled again. Uriah is just too good and loyal, in contrast to David, who is conniving and cunning. Uriah just doesn't do what he should to save David's hide. David understands that the penalty for adultery, even for the king, is stoning for both the man and woman committing adultery (see Deut. 22:22).

David has one more ploy up his sleeve—to just have Uriah killed. David sends Uriah back to war with a letter for Joab. Unwittingly, Uriah delivers his death warrant to his commander. David, unable to cover up his adultery, brings Joab into his plot to have Uriah killed on the front. Joab, ever David's henchman, carries out the deed by sending Uriah to the front line of battle, where he is inevitably killed along with other soldiers. The others become collateral damage in order not to draw suspicion that Uriah has been singled out for an execution. His death is seen as a consequence of and result of active duty. In war, there are casualties; that is the nature of war. Joab has now conspired with David to kill Uriah, and David makes sure Joab knows that he knows what the commander has done on his behalf. David sends Joab a message that he is not to worry himself over the matter—Joab is to keep on doing what he does best, fighting and winning battles (see 2 Sam. 11:25).

When David learns that a number of men have been killed in the war, he is upset until he hears that Uriah also dies in the battle. He understands now—Joab has carried out his orders and used the others to cover up David's ultimate goal to get rid of Uriah. When Bathsheba learns of her husband's death, she mourns. And surely she wonders what will happen to her—she's a pregnant widow. Talk about a dire situation—she is scandalized, with nowhere to go and no one to take care of her. We don't know if she suspects David's hand in this turn of events.

When her mourning period is over, David repeats the actions that got him into trouble in the first place—he sends for her and brings her back to the palace; only this time, he marries her. Again, we don't know how Bathsheba feels about any of this. She is silent in the text, except for her note to David. We learn that she has a son. It seems that David has gotten away with murder and that Bathsheba has been saved from shame and dishonor. Publicly, all is well with

David and Bathsheba. He has made an honest woman of Bathsheba. She is married to the king and has given birth to his son. We are alerted, though, in the very next verse that things are not going to end here:

> But the thing that David had done displeased [YHWH] . . . (2 Sam 11:27c)

Spiritually, despite public appearances, things are not well and someone will have to pay. The prophet Nathan rebukes David—David has violated Bathsheba, violated and set up Uriah, implicated Joab in his crimes, caused the demise of innocent soldiers—David's hands are dirty because he has overstepped the bounds of his power. David is chastised and he repents. His life is spared but his personal life never goes well after this incident. In fact, the child born to David and Bathsheba pays dearly for David's sins. The child becomes ill and dies. Notice here that Bathsheba is not named; she is the "wife of Uriah." She has been devalued, even as a daughter and wife, to indicate that the story is really about David and not her. We know that the child is a boy (2 Sam. 11:27), but even the child is referred to as "it" in 2 Samuel 12:15b—again, the story is about David, not Bathsheba or the child.

The death of the baby seems especially cruel and unjust, and God sanctions the death. We are tempted to hold God responsible for the child's death—why does God let an innocent child die while David is able to move on with his life? We have no answer for this question and we are left with an unflattering picture of God. But remember that the text focuses on David, who does not get away scott-free for his deeds. The death of this child is only the beginning of tragic events in David's domestic life. The text shows David's actions surrounding the child's fate—while the child is ill, David prays for the life of the child, fasts, and lies on the ground all night. These are signs of mourning; but when the child dies, David resumes his life. His action after the death of the child is puzzling; but it shows a change in David. Unable to change the course of the consequences for which he is responsible, David accepts the reality of death and moves on. All the while, Bathsheba is absent from the narrative. Only when the child dies does she reappear—David goes to comfort her and, in time, she conceives and gives birth to another son. For the first time, she is named without reference to Uriah; she is now David's wife. They name their second son Solomon, whose name in Hebrew is a derivative of "shalom," which means "peace" and "wholeness." His name points out the irony of the events that have led to his birth—far from it being a time of peace and wholeness, David has instigated a series of violent, cruel, and brutal events that include rape, murder, cover-up, and the death of innocent lives. The text, however, also raises the possibility that Solomon's birth is the beginning of a newness and wholeness; perhaps David's dirty past can be pushed aside and good things will now happen. We are told that God loves Solomon, and Nathan gives him a name, Jedidiah, indicating that Solomon is God's Beloved. Bathsheba remains silent in the text; however, she gives birth to at least three more sons for David: Shimea, Shobab, and Nathan.

The narrative returns to public life as the scene shifts to the exploits of Joab. Despite his military and political prowess, David's personal life continues a downward spiral. The next time we see Bathsheba, David is old, frail, sexually impotent, and bedridden (see 1 Kings 1:1–4). David's oldest son, Adonijah, wants to assume the throne under the advice and assistance of Joab and others of David's court. His attempt to seize power is only one of a series of his sons' quest for power.

Before Adonijah is crowned, however, the prophet Nathan approaches Bathsheba and seeks her help in landing the crown for Solomon. In dramatic fashion, Nathan informs

Bathsheba that she and Solomon are in danger. He tells the story of Adonijah as if he has already assumed the throne; and he lets Bathsheba know that Adonijah is the son of a rival wife. He is willing to conspire with her to make sure that Adonijah does not come into power:

> Have you not heard that Adonijah son of Haggith has become king and our lord David does not know it? Now therefore come, let me give you advice, so that you may save your own life and the life of your son Solomon. (1 Kgs 1:11–12)

Nathan coaches Bathsheba about what to say to David and assures her that he will corroborate her story. It is not clear if David ever promised the throne to Solomon; what is clear is that the line of succession is in question. Although Adonijah is the heir apparent as the oldest living son, Nathan wants to see Solomon on the throne, and apparently Bathsheba does too. In cahoots with the prophet Nathan, Bathsheba convinces an elderly, nearly dead David that he promised the throne to Solomon.

Her audience with David makes for great television—he is "very old"; his new young and beautiful concubine, Abishag, is with him but is ignored by his wife—what will happen? We can hardly wait to see how the story unfolds. Bathsheba, earlier silent and passive, is now a spitfire of a woman. She is verbal and creative in that she does not simply parrot Nathan's words; rather, she embellishes his words and gives David quite a story, one that evokes his guilt, highlights his decline, and suggests that he suffers from memory loss. David, who used to know everything (see 2 Sam. 14:20), has no idea what is happening these days. The younger David would have questioned Bathsheba's story, especially when Nathan gives him a different story. Bathsheba declares that David promised the throne to Solomon; Nathan asks if David ever, indeed, offered the throne to Adonijah. Poor

David—he not only does not catch the discrepancy in their stories, he doesn't even remember whether he offered the throne to anyone. Both Nathan and Bathsheba offer convincing arguments for making Solomon David's successor—they imply that Adonijah has not only plotted against David but also has gathered a group of rebels to support him, including David's commander-in-chief and chief priest, Joab and Zadok.

David finally takes decisive action and sends for Bathsheba, who left when Nathan arrived. He declares to her that Solomon will take the throne with his blessings. Bathsheba becomes queen mother, and she wields her own power in the machinations of the politics of the throne. Adonijah, realizing Bathsheba's influence over Solomon, seeks her help in reclaiming the throne—he asks her to ask Solomon to turn over David's concubine, Abishag, to him (see 1 Kings 2:13–18). Such action is seen as a direct attempt to usurp the throne. It is not clear why he asks for Bathsheba's help; surely, he must have known that Bathsheba understood the implication of such a request. Bathsheba plays along with Adonijah and agrees to speak to Solomon on his behalf. As she approaches Solomon, she is honored and respected by her son; he even has a throne for her placed on his right side. She relays Adonijah's request and, as expected, Solomon sees through the ruse and moves to remove all threats to his throne. Either knowingly or unknowingly, Bathsheba is instrumental in helping Solomon kill those who also sought the throne, including his half-brothers.

These episodes in 1 Kings cause us to reassess our judgment of Bathsheba. In 2 Samuel, she is silent except for her written message to David. She appears to be a victim of royal prerogative, power, and privilege. Here, though, she is active and in control of the situation. She pays obeisance to the king and totally ignores the beautiful Abishag. She improvises her speech to David and plays him expertly. Here, she is politically astute and manipulative. Here, she is calculating and works her plan to perfection—she gets what she wants from David.

Bathsheba has been characterized as a temptress who seduced a religious king to commit adultery. In addition, she marries her husband's murderer very soon after her widowhood. But what is her side of the story? We are not told anything about her thoughts or feelings. As a woman, she has no power to refuse the king; we are left to suppose that David likely rapes her. Furthermore, she is forced to marry her abuser. And she isn't David's only wife—he has many others and a number of concubines. On his dying bed, it isn't Bathsheba who is summoned to comfort him. Instead, Abishag is stationed at David's bedside to warm him. Instead of a life of ease and comfort, Bathsheba is in a palace filled with violence, intrigue, death, and family strife and discord.

We wonder if she is a victim of rape or a willing partner in her first encounter with David. The Bible describes him as "handsome and good looking"—a double whammy of sex appeal and perhaps too much to resist. We know he is a powerful man even before he is anointed king. Add that he has a strong spiritual side—he is certainly attractive to many women (and maybe even some men). It is suggested by some scholars that Bathsheba makes herself visible and available to David. Scholars say that she knew the king would be on the palace terrace so she scheduled her bath in the evening rather than in the morning, in a covert act of seduction. Other scholars support her cunning by stating how she had not gotten pregnant with Uriah. Having the king's son would certainly create a different future for her.

Women, however, are often blamed for men's sexual weaknesses and we ought not too quickly jump to hold her responsible for his actions. It is just as likely that David sees a woman he wants and, as king, he gets what he wants. He certainly pays the price for his lust.

We watch a transformed Bathsheba move from passive, silent victim to woman of many words and action. We can only imagine what is behind her transformation; whether she loves David or not, she is only one of many wives. There is no evidence that David ever wined and dined Bathsheba. We still don't know if she knows about David's hand in the death of her first husband, Uriah. On more than one occasion, she likely witnesses how cruel and brutal David can be. And David's family life certainly does not lend itself to romance and ease—his sons are wicked and crazy; David does not protect his daughters; and he finds himself fighting with his sons for the throne.

Bathsheba is used by a powerful ruler, widowed at the hands of the king, forced to marry her abuser and the murderer of her husband, left alone to mourn the death of her first child, and all but ignored as her second husband lays dying. She finds a way to secure her future and that of her children by making sure Solomon is named successor to the throne, and she initiates his action to eliminate all threats to his power. Bathsheba has been through a lot. She is not just a victim—she has grown into a wise woman who understands a power game and works to make the game work to her advantage. We don't know how her life would have unfolded had she not been bathing that evening when David was bored and lustful. As it stands, she emerges as a woman who makes the situation work for her. And who are we to blame her for that?

REFLECTION QUESTIONS

1. Do you think Bathsheba was raped or was a willing participant in her encounter with David? Explain your answer.

2. Why do you think women are held responsible for the weaknesses of men, especially in sexual matters?

3. Why do you think God allowed her firstborn child to die? How do you account for David's reaction to the child's death? How do you suppose Bathsheba reacted?

4. Have you ever found yourself the victim of powerful men? How did you handle the situation? What advice do you offer other women who are pawns in men's power games?

5. Where do you suppose Bathsheba's family and friends are? Why are they not mentioned in the text?

6. Why do you think the story of David and Bathsheba continues to generate interest? What aspects of their story seem most intriguing?

7. Has your opinion of Bathsheba changed as you have come to see her as a verbal and active participant in David's story?

8. What hinders or enhances you to be an active agent in your own life? What support can you offer to empower other women?

9. What do we learn about David in these episodes with Bathsheba? What do we learn about Bathsheba in her interactions with David and Nathan?

10. What do you think feminists and womanists have to say to Bathsheba about her life? Explain your answer.

6

RIZPAH
I Shall Not Be Moved

READ

2 Samuel 3:6–11, 21:1–13

FOCUS TEXT

Then Rizpah the daughter of Aiah took sackcloth, and spread it
on a rock for herself, from the beginning of harvest until rain fell
on them from the heavens; she did not allow the birds of the air
to come on the bodies by day, or the wild animals by night.
(2 Sam 21:10)

"Look at what they've done to my babies!" Rizpah is not a
well-known "bad girl." Her story is part of the extensive
David corpus, and she is easily overlooked. Rizpah is the
daughter of Aiah and is a concubine of King Saul, Israel's first
monarch. Rizpah bears two sons for Saul—Armoni and
Mephibosheth. After Saul's death, Abner claims her as his
concubine. Abner, the son of Ner and grandson of Abiel, is
Saul's cousin and his commander-in-chief. In claiming Rizpah,

Abner indicates his intention to assume the throne and his act is seen and interpreted as an attack against Saul and Saul's house. When Saul's son, Ishbosheth, objects to Abner's actions, Abner changes his allegiance from Saul to David.

Early in his reign, David presides during an extended famine. Ancient peoples believed that their fortunes depended on the quality of their relationships with their gods. For Israel, the nation prospers when ruler and people are obedient and faithful to God. Likewise, when they are disobedient, they suffer. Unfortunate or tragic events and circumstances are the result of some breach in the covenantal relationship with God. The immediate goal would be to repair the breach in the relationship. So, when Israel suffers an ongoing famine, David believes it is because of some lapse within the nation. We learn that the famine is due to Saul's broken oath with the Gibeonites, a group of non-Israelites who are promised asylum in Israel (see 2 Sam. 21:1–9). The Gibeonites are occupying the land when Joshua swoops in to claim the land. They manage to avoid extermination; Joshua spares them but makes them workers for the people of Israel (see Josh. 9:1–27).

As the famine stretches into the third year, David asks what retribution is needed. The Gibeonites do not ask for material goods like silver or gold; instead, they ask for the "house of Saul"—that is, they want to kill all remaining male members of Saul's family. David captures and hands over to the Gibeonites seven of Saul's descendants—two sons (Rizpah's sons, Armoni and Mephibosheth, not Jonathan's son with the same name) and five grandsons (Merab and her husband, Adriel's, five sons)—for a ritual execution. All are summarily executed and impaled at the beginning of the barley harvest in late spring. The Gibeonites leave the bodies in the open where they are exposed to wild animals and birds. The request of the Gibeonites provides a handy excuse for David to wipe out the remnants of Saul's dynasty. But by leaving the bodies exposed, David is complicit with an abomination. Of course, his inaction to bury the bodies raises serious questions: Why does David wait for three years before seeking an answer to the famine? Why does God reveal Saul's bloodguilt only to David? Why is this judgment given now instead of during Saul's reign? Why is there no mention of Saul's transgression before now? Why does David ask the Gibeonites what retribution is needed instead of asking God? Why does God require a bloody solution for Saul's act? Why does God allow innocent people to die of starvation? Again, so many questions and so few answers.

This turn of events is certainly convenient for David even though untold numbers of innocent people have died. David uses the unfortunate famine to rid himself of any threats to his power and throne. Even after his death, Saul's supporters still hold out hope that his house will be restored to power. But those hopes are dashed with the murder of Saul's remaining sons and grandsons. David does spare Jonathan's son, but he is disabled and poses no threat to David. Most seem to understand the need for the ritual execution—at least, no one in the text protests, and David is absolved of any guilt.

But then, there's Rizpah. She is filled with grief and refuses to leave the bodies unattended. She keeps a silent vigil over the bodies from the beginning of the barley harvest until the rains come—day after day, night after night, week in and week out—she stands watch over the bodies of her slain family members. From about April to October or November, night and day, she keeps watch over the bodies of these seven men. Word reaches David that Rizpah has staged a silent vigil over the bodies. David learns of her faithful watchfulness. We are not sure what finally motivates him to act, guilt or compassion. But he is smart enough to know that he has to do something and he has the bodies, along with those of Saul's and Jonathan's, properly buried. David has their bones interred in Saul's family plot in Zela, in the land of Benjamin. Despite his role in the death of Saul's house, David comes off smelling like a rose—how ironic that his reputation as a good guy remains intact.

Rizpah's situation is tragic for several reasons:

- Although she is identified as Saul's concubine, she is actually a secondary wife. Still she is not in charge of her own body. She is made available to the whims of the men who surround her—Saul and Abner.

- She is caught in a power struggle between Saul and Abner; there is no consideration of her feelings or of her body. She is a pawn, passed around at will by men who are seeking power over each other.

- She watches two of her sons mercilessly killed and mounted onto stakes. She is unable to give them a fitting burial and is reduced to watching their decaying bodies exposed to the elements and to predators—for months on end.

- She is a widow without the benefit of sons to care for her. In other words, she is a nonperson in the culture.

Rizpah has no political or military power. But her silent vigil is a slap in the face to those in power. Her silence speaks volumes to the brutish power structure and to the cruelty of the leaders, including David. Therefore, her vigil is a powerful act of defiance. All she does is sit—in the sunshine, in the gloom of night, in the still of the morning—she sits. So removed from the situation is David that he has to ask what Rizpah is up to; her presence is a reminder of the wrong the Gibeonites have done with the sanction of David and God. There are no excuses for leaving the bodies exposed. Her silence convicts the powerful men of the day and they are forced to think about their deeds—day in and day out.

Rizpah is a "bad girl" because she refuses to condone the wickedness of men in power. She never utters a word in the text; she alone keeps vigil—there are no girlfriends or family who join her. She manages short catnaps, no comfortable nights of restful sleep. Even when the rains come, she shelters as best she can—nothing, drenching rain nor scorching sun, sways her from her post. She sits as a witness to those who think they have power and might. Powerless, silent, defenseless, and alone, Rizpah sits over her dead and mourns. In her action, she speaks justice to power and makes a point: wrongs will be judged; injustice will be addressed; the guilty will pay.

REFLECTION QUESTIONS

1. Rizpah is able to sit and wait—this symbolizes her power. What is the source of her capacity to do nothing but sit and wait in silence?

2. What contemporary examples do you know of where women are making political statements when they seem to hold little or no power?

3. In what ways do women today empower themselves? How do you help empower women? Why is the empowerment of women important?

4. Do you consider yourself powerful? In what ways do you use your power? What is its source?

5. What are some ways people protest today? Do you think violent or nonviolent methods are more effective? Explain your answer.

6. What power is there in keeping a vigil? In what ways is keeping a vigil a political act today?

7. Do you think David is politically or spiritually motivated to finally bury the bones of Saul and his family?

8. Why do you think Saul's other wives and daughters do not join Rizpah in her vigil? Would you have joined her? Why or why not?

9. Why do you think God condones the murder of the seven men?

10. What words of comfort do you offer a mother who has lost her child?

HULDAH
Hard Words for Tough Times

READ

2 Kings 22:11–20, 2 Chronicles 34:19–28

FOCUS TEXT

So the priest Hilkiah, Ahikam, Achbor, Shaphan, and Asaiah
went to the prophetess Huldah the wife of Shallum son of
Tikvah, son of Harhas, keeper of the wardrobe; she resided in
Jerusalem in the Second Quarter, where they consulted her.
She declared to them, "Thus says [YHWH], the God of Israel;
. . . (2 Kings 22:14–15a)

*"How do I break this news to the ruler? He's such a good man,
too!"* Huldah is not as well known as some other "bad girls"
in the Bible. She is one of five women officially identified as
prophets listed in the Hebrew Bible, along with Miriam,
Deborah, Noadiah, and Isaiah's unnamed wife. Huldah lives
in Jerusalem during the reign of Josiah. She is married to a

minor temple official, Shallum, and is the daughter-in-law of Tikvah, the son of Harhas. Her husband is the keeper of the king's (priests') wardrobes. She is called upon to deliver a tough message during a hard time for Israel.

After King Solomon's reign, Israel faces uncertain times. Solomon learns nothing from his father about making the line of succession clear. A united nation under David and Solomon falls apart after Solomon's death. Solomon is crowned monarch under the shadow of Bathsheba and the prophet Nathan's shenanigans. Solomon starts well but falls short of the great expectations about his leadership. For the biblical narrator, Solomon's great crime is that he loves foreign women. In addition, Solomon exploits the people to complete his administrative decisions to expand the palace and to build the Temple. The unity among the tribes is tenuous, even under David's reign. Solomon doesn't do much to bring harmony to the nation, and shortly after his death his two sons fight for the throne.

Rehoboam and Jeroboam vie for leadership and end up ripping the nation apart. Israel consists of the ten northern tribes, who choose Jeroboam as their monarch. Judah consists of the tribe of Judah in Jerusalem, who chooses Rehoboam as their monarch. The strong powerhouse Israel is no longer the united nation David fought hard to construct. Each nation has its own history and line of monarchs. Leadership in the north, Israel, is chaotic and filled with intrigue and violence. Leadership in the south fares somewhat better because God promises David an eternal dynasty. The line of succession is a bit more predictable in Judah but this does not mean that all goes well for the nation. Each monarch is judged on how well he walks in the ways of David and by how obediently he follows God's statutes and commandments. As we can imagine, those rulers in the north do not fare well. They receive negative assessments while those in the south receive more positive assessments.

Judah is smaller and more geographically isolated than Israel. There are tensions between those who live in Jerusalem, the big city, and those who live in the outlying, rural areas. These tensions give rise to class stratification and division throughout the territory. The people continue to commit acts of idolatry and injustice. The rich and powerful disregard the poor, and monarchs just make matters worse. A young Josiah succeeds Amon as ruler in Judah following his servants' assassination of Amon after a mere two years in office. The assassins are in turn murdered, and Josiah is anointed king (see 2 Kings 21:19–24).

Josiah, a ruler whose heart is set on God and God's ways, sets about to rebuild Jerusalem and the Temple. He plans to pay workers a fair wage to set an example for other businesspersons in Jerusalem. Before the plan is implemented, Hilkiah, the high priest, is given a scroll discovered by some workers who are clearing out the clutter in the Temple. He hands the scroll over to Shaphan, the king's secretary. Shaphan lets Josiah know about the find and reads it to him. Josiah's reaction is dramatic—he tears his clothes as an act of mourning, perhaps indicating how seriously Judah has strayed from God's ways. He knows things are bad but he now realizes that things in Judah are really, really bad.

Neither Josiah nor his officials are sure if the scroll is authentic and needs to be interpreted. Josiah appoints an official board to find if the scroll is credible—Hilkiah the high priest, Ahikam son of Shaphan, Achbor son of Micaiah, Shaphan the secretary, and Asaiah the ruler's servant. This is a contingent of important leaders in Judah. This is no small matter for Josiah; the very life of the nation depends on the interpretation of the scroll. He sends his most trusted leaders and advisors to seek some answers. Interestingly enough, instead of consulting more prominent prophets like Jeremiah or Zephaniah, Josiah sends them to Huldah.

Huldah is carefully identified as a competent prophet and a loyal member of Josiah's extended court leadership. She confirms Josiah's worst fears: the impending doom and destruction of Jerusalem and the death of Josiah. The judgment is harsh because the people have disobeyed God and served idols. Her prophecy says it all: the people have abandoned God, have followed other gods, and have stirred up God's wrath (see 2 Kings 22:17). There is to be no reprieve from the consequences—Judah must pay for its transgressions. She prophesies that Josiah will not live to see the destruction of Judah; instead, he will die in relative peace.

The group of leaders does not question her prophecy and they give an honest report of her words to Josiah. Even Josiah takes her prophecy seriously, despite the harshness of her words. Huldah's gender is not an issue in this case, although she is identified in patriarchal terms as the wife of Shallum son of Tikvah, son of Harhas. Some suggest these names are dropped to indicate her loyalty to Judah. If harsh words must be spoken, they will come from someone who loves Judah and is loyal to the king. That is, Huldah the prophet will speak words of truth and not words to discourage or undermine the king's power. Josiah does not question the truth of her words nor does he seek out another prophet in the hope of hearing easier words of judgment.

Josiah, yet hopeful for a better outcome, institutes a massive religious and social reform that includes Jerusalem as well as local cultic centers throughout Judah. He begins by gathering the people, including the elders, the priests, the prophets, and all others in the nation. He reads the "book of the covenant," which is the same book Hilkiah had brought to Josiah. The monarch conducts a covenant renewal ritual, and the people recommit themselves to the covenant (see 2 Kings 23:1–3).

Josiah's reforms are comprehensive: Hilkiah, his associate priests, and the guardians of the Temple are commanded to cleanse the Temple of all traces of Baal, which are taken outside the city and burned. The houses of the male temple prostitutes are dismantled; the altars on the high places (alternative places of worship or sanctuaries outside the Temple) are torn down; the altar at Bethel is dismantled; all the shrines of the high places in Samaria (note that the destroyed nation Israel has by now been renamed Samaria; its inhabitants are no longer called Israelites but rather are called Samaritans. These changes occur after the Assyrians take over the Northern Kingdom in order to destroy Israel's very identity and existence). Josiah gathers all the priests of the high places and has them killed.

Josiah purges the land of idolatry and returns to Jerusalem. There, he reestablishes the Passover festival begun during the Exodus. Instead of celebrating the festival in individual homes, he establishes Jerusalem as the site for observing the Passover (which continues to the days of Jesus). Despite his zealous reform and purging, Josiah is not able to save Judah. And despite Huldah's prophecy that Josiah will die in peace, he does not. Josiah learns that Neco, the Pharaoh of Egypt, is meeting with the ruler of the Assyrians in an effort to thwart the aggressive moves of Babylon. Josiah wants to meet up with them at Megiddo, a major fortified city. Neco kills Josiah, whose body is taken back to Jerusalem, where he is buried in his family tomb. Josiah has a peace-filled burial and does not live long enough to see the destruction of Judah and the Temple, but the narrative is silent about the details of Josiah's demise. As it stands, Huldah's prophecy is true.

Huldah the prophet has no choice but to speak the words of God. Her speech follows the typical speech of other prophets: "Thus says [YHWH]. . . ." These words give credibility to her speech despite the dire predictions. She is a qualified prophet of God. No matter how much she wishes things would turn out differently, she must speak truth to power. Her credentials are not questioned and Josiah takes her words to heart. He does what he can, but the die has been cast. Both prophet and monarch recognize there is no hope—Judah will fall.

The work of the prophet in ancient Israel was complex and layered. The work ranged from sharing the gifts of poetry, song, and dance to teaching the Torah, in addition to making social commentary and predictions. The prophet mediated communication between God and people. Huldah was considered a full-fledged prophet. Her work was in the public arena. That Josiah and his leadership team consulted her about the "law" or Torah implies that Huldah did more than make predictions about the future. She was also a teacher of the law. Her understanding of the law led her to speak a harsh word in the midst of national crisis.

Huldah had a tough job—how to break bad news to the power brokers in Judah. She comes across in the text as courageous and self-assured. Surely her heart was breaking as she saw into the future of her beloved Judah. Her words moved Josiah to make sweeping changes despite the bad news. We do not know what happened to her or her family. We do not know how much of the destruction she saw first-hand. We do not know if she shared her experience or prophecy with Jeremiah or the other prophets. We know that her words moved the ruler to make sweeping changes and reforms even though they seemed futile. How did she go on living knowing that nothing would change the outcome? It would have been easier for her to lie and paint a rosier picture for Josiah and his delegation.

But Huldah stands in the prophetic tradition—speaking hard words for tough times.

REFLECTION QUESTIONS

1. How do you think Huldah reacts to her call to be a prophet?

2. How do you understand the terms "prophet" and "prophetic speech" in the Bible and in contemporary life?

3. Why do you think Josiah seeks the advice of a woman prophet?

4. Are there modern-day prophets? Who are they? What are their messages?

5. Do you have prophetic tendencies? How do you know?

6. If you disagree with a prophet's messages, do you still consider them prophetic? Explain your answer.

7. What does it take to speak an unpopular word to leaders and community today?

8. What areas of your life, personally and publicly, need a word of prophecy?

9. Why do you think neither Huldah nor Josiah asked God for a reprieve for Judah?

10. What is your prayer for the United States?

8

A CRIPPLED WOMAN
Do You See What I See?

READ

Luke 13:10–17

FOCUS TEXT

When [Jesus] laid his hands on her, immediately she stood up straight and began praising God. (Luke 13:13)

"Who is that calling me and what does he want?" The "bent-over" or crippled woman is among those nameless and voiceless women we find throughout the Bible. What is interesting about her story is that she doesn't ask for or seek a cure for her condition. Jesus sees her and performs a miracle—she is able to stand up straight for the first time in eighteen years. Her response to her healing is to praise God, although we are not privy to her actual words of praise.

The book of Luke has been considered the Gospel for women because more women appear in this book than the other Gospels. Luke often balances stories about men with stories about women and implies there is gender equality. In Luke, women have voice, take action, and serve as models for faithfulness and discipleship.

Feminist, womanist, and postcolonial scholars, however, are reluctant to give Luke two thumbs up when it comes to his portraits of women. Although he gives us more women in various roles, Luke continues to control and constrain women. Women who speak are often corrected or chided by Jesus. Women receive blessings, miracles, and healings from Jesus, but those who are silent and passive are praised. Women are not identified specifically as prophets, teachers, evangelists, or missionaries in Luke even though they function in these ways.

On the surface, we might conclude that this story is not really about the woman—she is a foil in the conflict between Jesus and his opponents. But there are clues in the text that this story serves a dual purpose: first, it is a story of liberation for all who are oppressed and bent over; and second, it is a challenge to institutional structures and systems that devalue humanity and human needs. The context of her story is at one of synagogues on the Sabbath. Before she ever appears, we are suspicious that something out of the ordinary will happen. Whenever we find Jesus teaching in a synagogue on a Sabbath, our antennas perk up because trouble can't be far behind.

Her presence at the synagogue on the Sabbath is especially important to the biblical storyteller. Despite her crippling condition that renders her ritually unclean, she makes her way with others into the synagogue. Her presence may indicate how common it was for women to participate in synagogue worship; perhaps some even were leaders of worship. She doesn't allow her crippling condition to keep her away from the synagogue, where she joins others in prayer, praise, and ritual.

She is doubled over and has difficulty walking. Her angle of vision is downward and it has been eighteen years since she has lifted her face to be kissed by the sun and to feel raindrops on her cheeks. Because she is bent over, she surely has difficulty managing basic human processes—going to the bathroom, bathing, dressing herself. Because of her condition, she surely has a challenge sexually, and in household chores such as hanging up the laundry and cooking. She must always ask for help reaching for things on shelves. Because of her handicapping condition, she surely finds it difficult to dance, to greet others, to hug her children.

It is likely she didn't even see Jesus because her attention is focused on the ground just below her. She is one of three people in the Bible who are healed without first making a request; the others are Peter's mother-in-law (Matt. 8:14–15) and the widow of Nain (Luke 7:11–17). It may be that she understands that no healings will happen on the Sabbath. Jesus sees her and calls to her—in this instance, we are reminded of Hagar whom God finds, sees, and calls. Jesus takes the initiative to lead the woman to a different status.

The woman in this episode is seen by Jesus, who calls to her, "Woman." Jesus uses the same term in referring to his mother—it is a generic yet respectful term. He beckons her. She is probably confused; with the crowd heading into the synagogue, she can't see faces. Is someone actually speaking to her? She follows the direction of the voice until she sees the feet of Jesus. She has not said a word and we cannot be sure she even knows who Jesus is.

Before she can form a question in her mind, Jesus makes a startling declaration that frees her from her ailment. Then he does an even more startling thing—he lays hands on her. This act is usually performed in the context of prayer and blessing. Jesus breaks all kinds of conventions when he interacts with the woman.

First, it is not proper for Jewish men to deal with women not in their own family. Second, he deals with her in the holiest of public spaces, the synagogue. Third, he deals with an unclean woman. The belief of those days was that handicapping conditions were the result of demons or satanic forces. These forces were supposed to cause all manner of maladies and disorders. Amazingly, the woman makes her way to the synagogue despite her condition and the presumed cause of it. Fourth, Jesus touches her—in public, knowing that she is ritually unclean. Any one of these offenses would be enough to condemn Jesus and bring shame upon him.

But Jesus ignores convention and seizes an opportunity to change the life of one person. A Jewish teacher heals her, unexpectedly and surprisingly. She has no idea how her life will change by her encounter with Jesus. Without fanfare or dramatic pause, she stands upright for the first time in eighteen years. Can you imagine what she must feel in that moment? For the first time in nearly two decades, she is able to look at someone, eyeball to eyeball. And the first person she sees is Jesus—of all people, he is her first sight as an upright person. Her response is joy—a joy that leads her to praise God. Her focus remains on God—the God who has sustained her for eighteen years is now also the God who heals. Jesus does not stop her praise nor does he correct her conclusion.

And this is where the story should end—a woman with a crippling condition finds healing as she goes about her normal activities. At the synagogue on the Sabbath—what better place and time for a healing miracle? What better place than the house of God, where women and men gather to pray and give honor to God? There is no better place to celebrate God's grace and healing mercies than the synagogue on the Sabbath.

But instead of her story ending on a high note, the action abruptly shifts to one of conflict and controversy. One of the synagogue leaders is indignant and upset that Jesus has violated the law that no work be done on the Sabbath. The leader tries to shame Jesus for his act of healing, but we know Jesus never backs down from a challenge.

Jesus gives as good as he gets—and calls the synagogue leader and his sympathizers hypocrites. He accuses them of being more compassionate with their oxen and donkeys than with a woman who has been bound by Satan for eighteen years. Jesus complies with the conventional thinking about ailments and infirmities being the work of Satan and demonic forces. In his response, Jesus shifts the shame from himself and onto the synagogue leader and the others who think Jesus has transgressed the law. In this male-dominated conflict and conversation, the woman is all but forgotten. The synagogue leader is more concerned about Jesus's actions than he is about the woman's healing. In fact, his issue is not about her healing; rather he is bugged out about the timing. He states that healings are fine—as long as they happen on the other six days of the week. The Sabbath is to be kept holy by not working. Both Jesus and his opponents take for granted that the woman's condition renders her unclean and an outcast.

Jesus, though, understands that the reign of God is breaking into the current reality. And right now is the right time for healing. He does not hesitate and even stops his teaching to heal the woman. Jesus states his mission clearly:

"The Spirit of the [Holy One] is upon me,
    because[God] has anointed me
        to bring good news to the poor.
[God] has sent me to proclaim release to the captives
    and recovery of sight to the blind,
        to let the oppressed go free,
to proclaim the year of the [Holy One]'s favor."

And [Jesus] rolled up the scroll, gave it back to the attendant, and sat down. The eyes of all in the synagogue were fixed on him. Then he began to say to them, "Today this scripture has been fulfilled in your hearing." (Luke 4:18–21)

His work includes healing—making women and men whole in mind, body, and spirit. In Jesus's eyes, eighteen years is long enough to suffer the indignity of being an outcast. Eighteen years is long enough to be labeled unclean. Eighteen years is long enough to see only the ground. Why wait for tomorrow when Jesus can do something now? Jesus shames his opponents by highlighting the woman's value and worth. Jesus continues, accusing the synagogue leader and others of caring more about their farm animals than about the woman. He hammers home his point by declaring the woman a "daughter of Abraham." Not only is she more important than animals, she also is part of God's family. She, who has been shunned and looked down upon, outcast and unclean, now has a cherished place in God's household.

Jesus pulls a fast one on his opponents—he heals an individual, restoring her to wholeness and community. In addition, he challenges the very tradition that diminishes her personhood. He reinterprets the law about the Sabbath so that people are valued over rules. Jesus reminds the leaders that the spirit of the law is greater than the letter of the law. The point of the law is to dictate the character of community—mutuality, cooperation, love, and reverence for God. In their zeal to keep the law, the leaders have lost sight of what they themselves should be doing—rejoicing with the woman that God is alive and still in the healing business.

The lesson is not lost on the crowd—those gathered at the synagogue recognize that God is still working to bring persons to wholeness and to bring community into fullness. Individual healings are good, but communal health is even better. What looks like a simple healing on the surface is actually a challenge to the powers and principalities, structures and systems that keep persons burdened, bowed down, and bent over. Jesus sees the woman and sees an opportunity for an object lesson. How can he teach about freedom and wholeness and let this woman remain bent over and crippled?

Despite the reprimand from the synagogue leader, Jesus does the right thing for the right reasons. The synagogue leader's job is to monitor the crowd to make sure that the Sabbath is rightly observed. He may be a man of great compassion and caring, but his job is to make sure there is order in the synagogue. He and his cohorts are shamed because they place order above compassion. Jesus reminds them of what is truly important, and they are put in their places by his indictment that renders them "hypocrites."

Jesus is on the woman's side and does not rescind her healing. For many, this story is symbolic of freedom for women—freedom from conditions and situations that leave them bowed down and bent over. The story is symbolic of women who are finally released from various burdens and afflictions that prevent them from standing tall and empowered. The story is emblematic of women who are no longer limited and fenced in by doctrines, creeds, and policies.

This "bad girl," however, is not just a mirror for women. She is a mirror for the masses of humanity that find themselves in narrow and limited situations, conditions, and circumstances. She symbolizes all who suffer and must find ways to survive in cultures that don't care about them. She embodies the injustice that is all too prevalent in the world.

By healing her and confronting the leaders, Jesus shows us what discipleship is about—caring for persons and working to bring justice to those places where people are bent over and ignored. This episode with the crippled woman is Jesus's last appearance in a synagogue in Luke's Gospel. Jesus uses the occasion to defy social conventions by elevating the woman as he affirms her place in God's realm and household. She is daughter of Abraham and therefore has a claim as Abraham's progeny. Furthermore, Jesus demotes the honor of the synagogue leader and his sidekicks by challenging their interpretation of law and their living outside of the spirit of the law they are charged with maintaining.

The woman goes about her business, and Jesus stops teaching to help the sister out. But her story is overshadowed by male voices and tensions. She is not named in the text nor does she speak. She is all but invisible except as a ploy for the men to enact their shame and honor game. Her presence indicates that women regularly attended synagogue worship, and she did not allow her handicapping condition keep her from praising God. Her response to her healing is one of joy and ongoing rejoicing. She is a model of faithfulness for us—whether sick or well, she understands that worship is the center of her spirituality. She has continued to worship God for the eighteen years of her infirmity; nothing will deter her from worshiping God.

This bad girl never utters a word we can hear. We know that, in her upright position, she praises God. We know that the community rejoices with her—for God is still working to straighten bent bodies, to mend broken spirits, to keep hope alive, and to make a place for everyone in God's realm that has no end. Jesus has set her free from crippling, imprisoning conditions—by doing so, God heals her physically and enables her to stand tall and proud. Further, Jesus returns her to the community that has marginalized her because of her condition. In healing the woman, God assures us, through Jesus, that we have a place—a place of honor and dignity in God's household. Thanks be to God for this nameless, voiceless bad girl who shows us that God's mercy and faithfulness is available to and for all!

REFLECTION QUESTIONS

1. What do you imagine the woman says after she realizes she is healed? How do you think her family and friends react to her healing?

2. From what troubles or situation do you need freedom? How do you pray about these concerns? Explain.

3. Who are the "bent-over" people in your midst? What are the causes for their "infirmities"?

4. Is it possible to balance doing one's job and expressing concern and compassion for others? What helps or hinders the balance?

5. Do you believe inequities and injustice are inevitable? Explain your answer.

6. What are you doing politically, socially, economically, and religiously to help people stand up tall?

7. This woman has an intense encounter with Jesus. What in your life needs Jesus's attention?

8. What is the role of community in one's sense of well-being and health?

9. Have you ever felt disempowered? How did you deal with the situation? What does wholeness mean for you? What does freedom mean for you? How does your answer differ from the answers your family or friends might give?

10. In what ways are church doctrines, creeds, and traditions life-giving? How are they life-denying?

9

THE SYROPHOENICIAN WOMAN
Struggles, Slurs, and Salvation

> **READ**
>
> Matthew 15:21–28
> Mark 7:24–30
>
> **FOCUS TEXTS**
>
> She said, "Yes, Lord, yet even the dogs eat the crumbs that fall from their masters' table." (Matt. 15:27)
>
> But she answered him, "Sir, even the dogs under the table eat the children's crumbs." (Mark 7:28)

"So Jesus—bring it on; I've got something for you!" The story of this unnamed woman is a candidate for passages we wish were not in the Bible. Both Mark and Matthew tell her story, each from a particular perspective. The basic story seems simple: a desperate mother pleads with Jesus to heal her demon-possessed daughter. After initially refusing to help her, Jesus insults her and her people before relenting and

healing the daughter. The story is multilayered and complex and poses a host of challenges. Among the many difficulties, first we must decide which version of the story to explore.

Mark is the first to include the story, and it is clear that Matthew appropriates and reworks the story. If we read the two versions side by side (as we can in *Gospel Parallels: A Comparison of the Synoptic Gospels*), we see some critical differences between them. Mark's is the shorter version, and the main action takes place inside a private home. Jesus is seeking relief from the crowds and wants to hide out. Mark places this episode after Jesus has fed the five thousand, walked on water, and taught about purification. The woman's identity is ethnically and politically highlighted—a Gentile, born a Syrophoenician. Her background is associated with wealth and materialism (David and Solomon imported lumber and craftspersons from Tyre and Sidon to build the royal palace and the Temple; see 2 Sam. 5:11, 1 Kings 5 and 7). As a Jew, Jesus is to have nothing to do with the woman although he is in Gentile territory. She bows down at Jesus's feet and begs him to heal her daughter. We don't hear her voice until Jesus rebuffs her request for the healing of her daughter. Even though he refuses to address her immediate concern, Jesus softens his rebuff by stating there will come a time when those outside of the house of Israel will be considered ("Let the children be fed first . . ." Mark 24:27). She comes right back at Jesus by turning his metaphor ("the dogs") on its ear—she is quick and bold in her retort to him. Jesus hears her words and sends her home to a healed child. She leaves with the hope that Jesus has kept his word—when she arrives home, she finds her daughter healed.

In contrast to Mark's barebones rendering, Matthew elaborates and expands the story by adding dramatic touches. In Matthew, Jesus has been rejected by his hometown folks, John the Baptist has been beheaded, Jesus has been followed by the crowds, and he has fed the five thousand. He is exhausted and seeks solitude. Matthew, however, places this story in a public setting and creates a substantial conversation among the woman, Jesus, and the disciples. There is high tension in Matthew's version. He identifies the woman only as a "Canaanite," which brings memories of the idolatrous and warring inhabitants of the land God had promised to Abraham and his progeny. Her identity carries religious as well as sociopolitical overtones. In addition, she causes a ruckus by shouting the title used by those who are outcasts and marginalized in Palestine, "Son of David." Of course, the title makes it clear that Jesus is connected to the Jews and not to those outside that circle. Jesus ignores her and his disciples urge him to send her away—they want her to stop embarrassing them with her wild and passionate pleas. It is not clear whether Jesus answers her directly or speaks to the disciples so that she overhears his response. His words are harsher here than in Mark because he does not imply that the Gentiles will have any part of God's redeeming work, "I was sent only to the lost sheep of the house of Israel." His reply doesn't stop her—she moves in front of Jesus and kneels down, impeding his steps. As he tries to get away from her, she blocks his path and begs him to help her (and we assume by helping her, he actually helps her daughter). Jesus and the woman then have a direct conversation while the disciples are silent. Jesus praises her faith and lets her know that her daughter is healed.

Despite the differences between the stories, there are some similarities that should not be missed. The first is that Jesus himself crosses the boundaries of what is acceptable when he enters the region of Tyre and Sidon. The region symbolizes the margin where differences are highlighted and people are pitted against each other. At the margins, it is not "us" and "we" but rather "them" and "those people." At the margins, people are distinguished by their differences—history, tradition, worldview, and rituals—there are tensions, challenges, and even violence at the margins. Jesus breaks protocols within the Jewish tradition but now he breaches the acceptable by placing himself in "enemy" territory, among the Gentiles.

Second, this woman has the audacity to approach Jesus to request a healing. She is a woman, a foreign woman, a woman not connected to a male authority figure, and the mother of a demon-possessed child, which also makes her ritually unclean. She has so many strikes against her—and she isn't even from the house of Israel. What nerve! And that brings us to the third point—she has no right to claim any kind of blessing from Jesus. Jesus's mission is only to the lost among the Jews. His work with his own people is exhausting and frustrating without adding the dimension of dealing with non-Jews. So Jesus is within his mission to refuse her request. We are a bit surprised at how easily Jesus dismisses her—he ignores and issues a slur when he does respond to her. In this episode, Jesus displays just how much a product of his time and place he is. He cannot avoid his social location and he seems okay with that.

This woman, however, is not to be put off. It is not clear where she gets her nerve from—is it from her privileged position in the region or is it the desperation of a mother who fears for the life of her child? Whatever her foundation, she insists that Jesus deal with her—the religious, social, and political barriers do not matter. If he is a healer, he should heal anyone who needs it. If he is a teacher, he should teach whoever will listen and hear. In other words, she challenges Jesus to be . . . Jesus.

He refers to her and her kind as "dogs." His slur raises all kinds of questions for those who have been taught that he practices radical inclusivity, treats all with dignity and respect, and advocates for the outcast and marginalized. It is suggested that she and Jesus bring their own cultural understandings to this metaphor. For Jesus, dogs are mixed breed mongrels that have food thrown at them. It is generally agreed among scholars that the Jews were not great pet-lovers. Dogs were seen as dirty and wild animals that canvassed the streets looking for food. They were not allowed in the house and certainly not near food. Jewish dietary and cleanliness laws and rituals would prohibit the inclusion of dogs in the household.

On the other hand, the Canaanites considered dogs to be part of the family, where they were allowed to eat table scraps. Dogs were allowed to play with the children and were welcomed inside the home. She uses her social location to help Jesus understand his mission: does God love all people who believe or not? Are you inclusive and welcoming or not? Do you believe others can come under the grace of your God or not?

She challenges Jesus in the same way he has challenged his opponents. She knows about Jesus and knows his teaching; she has taken his words and teachings to heart and hears a word of liberation and grace for her and her people. Who is Jesus to deny the power of God's words to heal, teach, convert, and redeem? She is not passive or "ladylike" in her approach—she is bold, bodacious, loud and, in this case, right! She challenges Jesus to practice what he preaches because he preaches power, regardless of who hears the message. At the margins and borders, the woman challenges Jesus to expand his vision, mission, ministry, and audience. She crosses the lines of propriety—she is not placed within a patriarchal framework, is not placed within a Judeo-Christian context, and is not placed within the parameters of acceptable female behavior. She speaks and talks back—she is no wallflower, silent and passive. She makes Jesus deal with her, even if it means blocking his path.

She is not intimidated and will not be ignored—whether Jesus heals her daughter or not, she will be heard and reckoned with by him. And yes, she will accept his slur; she may even be thinking the childhood defense familiar to many of us today: sticks and stones may break my bones, but words will never hurt me. She will hear his slur but she does not accept that as the last word. She may not yet be at God's table, but everything Jesus has preached and taught implies that she will, one day. She has words, Jesus has words, and she has more words. We know, of course, that words do hurt. Even Jesus knows this—perhaps, this is why he relents and reconsiders his interaction with her. Not only does Jesus hear her words, he hears the faith behind them. She begs Jesus to heal her daughter from a position of belief and trust that Jesus can do something. She is a desperate mother who watches helplessly as her daughter convulses, flails, thrashes about like a scene out of the film *The Exorcist*. She believes that Jesus can heal her daughter and she is up to the verbal sparring that Jesus initiates.

Her courage and audacity open the Jesus movement to folks regardless of racial, ethnic, and religious locations. Those who believe will have a place in God's household— old barriers are torn down. The Syrophoenician woman is a bad girl—she defies decorum and protocol on religious, ethnic, and gender levels. She is focused, determined, and borderline rude in her begging for Jesus to heal her daughter. She is courageous, assertive, and shameless in her persistence. Jesus does not back down from this strong woman and interprets her demeanor as evidence of great faith. He shows how to argue and how to lose graciously.

Because of her willingness to engage Jesus in conversation, she opens a new dimension of understanding and mission for Jesus. Because of her faith, she expands God's table to include even more who are labeled unworthy, outcast, and marginalized. She symbolizes the opening for Gentiles to join both the Markan and Matthean communities of faith after Jesus's resurrection. Further, she gives embodiment to the inclusion of women leaders in those communities, moving from the margins into the center of the faith community. She also teaches us what to do in a world where inequities and injustices abound—some have multicourse meals, while others have crumbs; some name and claim the center, while others are forced to the borders and margins; some live in mansions, while others have no shelter. But in God's household and economy, the haves and have-nots are reversed, and there is plenty good room for all at God's table, where the feast is bountiful.

REFLECTION QUESTIONS

1. What do you learn about Jesus in this episode with the Syrophoenician/Canaanite woman that is surprising? Does this knowledge enhance or hinder your faith in Jesus? Explain.

2. In what ways are you like the Syrophoenician/Canaanite woman? Explain your answer.

3. How do you react to Jesus's abrupt refusal to assist the woman? In what ways do you refuse to help others?

4. What has been your experience of marginalization? On what bases have you been excluded? How do you handle such situations?

5. Have you ever been the recipient of a racial or gender slur? Describe the circumstance and your reaction to it. Is there anything you can do to prevent future incidents?

6. Who are the "Syrophoenicians/Canaanites" in your midst? Do you welcome or exclude them? Explain how.

7. How do you accept defeat? Are you pleased with your reaction to losing? Why or why not?

8. What is the line between persistence and annoyance? What should the guidelines be for civil discourse, exchange, and disagreements?

9. Identify one or two important social issues. What stand have you taken on these issues? What empowers you to take a strong stand on these issues?

10. How far are you willing to go to support a loved one? Explain.

IO

MARTHA AND MARY
In the Midst of Tears, Standing on the Promises

READ

Luke 10:38–42
John 11:1–44

FOCUS TEXTS

But Martha was distracted by her many tasks; so she came to [Jesus] and asked, "Lord, do you not care that my sister has left me to do all the work by myself? Tell her then to help me." (Luke 10:40)

Jesus said to [Martha], "I am the resurrection and the life. Those who believe in me, even though they die, will live, and everyone who lives and believes in me will never die. Do you believe this?" She said to him, "Yes, Lord, I believe that you are the Messiah, the Son of God, the one coming into the world." (John 11:25–27)

"What's up with Jesus? I think something horrible is going to happen to him!" In Luke, we find the story of a family close to Jesus's heart. The family consists of two sisters and a brother: Martha, Mary, and Lazarus. They live in Bethany

and Jesus enjoys warm hospitality in their home. Bethany is about two miles outside of Jerusalem; this geographic detail will hold special meaning when we explore the Gospel of John text. We are not told how Jesus meets them or how they come to be such close friends and partners in ministry.

During a visit to their home, Jesus is teaching and enjoying the family's hospitality. The sisters are so different: Martha is busy bustling around to make sure all things are in order; her sister, on the other hand, is sitting at Jesus's feet listening to his teaching. And therein lies the rub—Martha expresses concern that Mary is not doing her fair share of the work. At least, that's how the story has been interpreted. There are some interesting nuances, though, that make this episode much more intriguing. The women display different styles of discipleship and this creates tension between them.

This text has been interpreted to highlight the different ways persons can follow Jesus. Martha welcomes Jesus and his followers into her home. Martha's way is the active and frenetic style. Mary's is the contemplative, passive style. The details of the story, however, shed a different light on the story. Martha's work of hospitality and welcoming is described as *diakonia*, usually associated with ministry or service as an act of faith. It is the word used to describe the work and service of the twelve (male) disciples. Scholars believe that Martha is the leader of a house-church and performs the duties of a disciple and those related to hospitality. She is a doer of God's word. Her *public* ministry is problematic in the Gospel of Luke; Luke's community is struggling with the leadership of women as well as the stress that goes with public leadership. It is not entirely clear why Martha is vexed in the text—is it the burden of leadership? The many tasks of hospitality? The lack of help to get the work done? Whatever her motivation, Martha wants Jesus to solve her problem and asks him to make Mary help with the work. Jesus, as the teacher and authority figure, behaves as a parent dealing with squabbling youngsters. Jesus chastises Martha instead of making Mary help. It seems as though Jesus is devaluing Martha's work and leadership and elevating Mary's.

Mary, on the other hand, has the "better part." She is a listener, a student, and operates in a passive way. Is Luke, or his community, trying to say that women make a "better" contribution when they are quiet, reserved, and hearers, rather than doers, of the word? For Luke, the appropriate place for women is in the home rather than in public spaces.

Luke, although he names the women and gives them voice and agency, puts the women in tension with each other. We are left to choose the "better" part—is it doing the word or merely hearing the word? According to this text, the passive style is valued. And Jesus, who has been a champion for the marginalized, praises the passive woman and seems to condone the private role of discipleship. This seems contrary to previous teachings where Jesus encourages both hearing and doing the word and work of discipleship. Luke, often touted as the feminist biblical writer, shows us that perhaps our accolades are not entirely merited. Luke pits the two women against each other and has them seek advice from a male authority figure. Neither seems free enough to operate on her own—Martha's words to Jesus are snippy, "*make* her help me!" Mary doesn't offer to help—she continues to sit at Jesus's feet. Jesus doesn't praise or affirm Martha's leadership but instead gives Mary permission to dismiss her leadership contribution.

As we read this story today, we ought not be too quick to choose one way of discipleship over another. Jesus seems to criticize Martha's attitude, not her work. He addresses her anxiety and agitation rather than the quality of her service. Maybe Jesus is calling for her (and us) to go with the flow of ministry and mission rather than fretting over whether things are perfect. What the episode highlights is that the work of ministry needs both doers and hearers—effective leadership means extending hospitality, learning the faith tradition, and embodying the traditions by engaging in ministry and service. There are times to be active and times to be quiet. Perhaps the women embody a fuller sense of what discipleship is about—it's not a matter of either/or but rather both/and. Effective leadership is a balance between reflection and action; we must think and do; hear and implement. Rather than pit reflective and active disciples against each other, we are encouraged to see how both modes contribute to fruitful ministry, service, and mission.

In shifting to the Gospel of John, we see a different side to Martha and Mary. The episode in John 11 is the last sign of Jesus's public ministry. The raising of Lazarus from death only appears here. When Lazarus becomes ill, the sisters are convinced that Jesus can heal him and they send for Jesus. Jesus procrastinates and shows up four days after Lazarus dies. A common belief during that time was that the soul stayed with the body until the fourth day, when it departed forever. So after four days, there is no doubt that Lazarus is dead and that his body has already started decaying. The customary mourning ritual is in full force—friends and neighbors gathering at the family's home and engaging in animated and loud weeping.

Martha leaves the mourning and runs out to meet Jesus; she leaves the privacy of her home to meet him as he approaches. In the Luke passage, both Martha and Mary are homebound. Here, we see Martha leaving her home and running out to meet Jesus—she is proactive and initiates a conversation with him. In her pain and disappointment at his delay, Martha meets Jesus with some harsh words, "if you had been here, my brother would not have died." She believes Jesus's delay has prevented her brother's healing. She accuses Jesus of neglect but she leaves open the possibility that something can yet be done for Lazarus, "But even now,

I know that God will give you whatever you ask. . . ." Martha leaves the fate of Lazarus in Jesus's hands rather than state her desire to see her brother alive again.

Jesus offers words of comfort and assures her that she will see her brother again. Martha responds with the theological understanding of her time: that she will see her brother at the general resurrection on the last day of existence and creation. You may recall that early Israel did not belief in life after death (see Psa. 115:17); the soul went to an underworld (Sheol) to wait for God's final judgment. As the nation and its theology developed, the concept of a general resurrection evolved (see Isa. 26:19 and Dan. 12:2). Resurrection was to be a communal event and persons would undergo a complete and total change.

In his theological exchange with Martha, Jesus utters one of his "I am" sayings: "I am the resurrection and the life." The promise of resurrection and life is fulfilled in Jesus—those who live and believe in Jesus will never die because he opens the way for an eternal relationship with God and those who believe in God. Jesus wants to make sure Martha understands his words and he asks if she believes what he has said.

Her response is unequivocal—not only does she believe his words, but also she believes that he is the Messiah! Her confession of faith parallels that of Peter in Matthew 16:15–16:

> [Jesus] said to [the disciples], "But who do you say that I am?" Simon Peter answered, "You are the Messiah, the Son of the living God."

This is the statement of faith—from the lips of a woman! Martha, a leader among those who follow and support Jesus and his ministry, sets the standard for faith. Ever the teacher and leader, she goes back to her home to let Mary know that Jesus wants to see her. This time, Martha has heard Jesus and confessed her faith in him as the Messiah. Note that Martha tells Mary about Jesus in private. In her excitement, Mary runs out to meet Jesus, too. Her interaction with Jesus mirrors her sister's, except she kneels down before Jesus as a sign of respect. But she chastises Jesus, too, and does so in the presence of the mourners who are following after her on the road. Jesus reacts with compassion, pity, and love—he weeps. Jesus expresses his grief with total abandon and without regard to the reaction of others. The crowd's reaction is mixed; some see his public display of mourning as a sign of his love for Lazarus; others are resentful because he waited, too late to be of any help to Lazarus.

Jesus goes to Lazarus' tomb and asks the stone covering the opening to be moved away. He calls in a loud voice for Lazarus to come out. And miraculously, Lazarus emerges from the tomb still wrapped in his burial clothes. The resurrection event sealed the deal against Jesus—some believed in him; others went off to tell his opponents. When Jesus's opponents heard the news, they conspired to bring Jesus to death.

In his last work of ministry, Jesus is surrounded by two "bad girls," Martha and Mary. Both women have been supporters of Jesus and his work. Martha, already a leader in her own right, confesses faith that Jesus is the One sent by God whom John the Baptist foretold. Her confession paves the way for the inclusion of women as leaders and teachers in the Jesus movement. Together, Martha and Mary give us a fuller picture of what it means for women to be followers of Christ—each brings her gifts and personality to the Jesus movement. There is room for the active types and for the more contemplative types.

Both women are verbal, intelligent, and active. Martha is outspoken and seems to enjoy a good debate. It is easy to cast her as a petty, faultfinding, jealous woman. Martha, however, highlights the stress of being a leader and recognizes the importance of teamwork. In addition, she is clear headed and articulate about her faith and service. Mary consistently shows reverence for Jesus, even if her respect does not always result in action. Each brings her whole self to faith and is theologically engaged. In Luke, we see the sisters in conflict with each other and Martha seeking validation from Jesus. In John, we see Martha's take-charge personality as she runs out to meet Jesus and engages him in a theological conversation. Jesus does not shy away from her as he reveals who he is to her. She believes and confesses her faith. We are left to wonder how Martha's ministry and leadership change after her confession and after witnessing the resurrection of her brother. Mary is portrayed as an eager student who is content to sit and listen to Jesus. In John, she is more active, leaving her home to find Jesus, and kneeling in reverence before him. We don't know if her ministry changes after the events surrounding Lazarus. And what of Lazarus? What must it be like for him—once dead and now alive? Martha and Mary are two bad girls who mirror and reflect back to each other (and to us) aspects that are missing in the other. Instead of seeing the sisters as competitors, we should see them as two sides of the same coin and work towards deeper relationships, greater wholeness, and greater mutuality in our faith community.

REFLECTION QUESTIONS

1. Martha is the leader of a house church. What roles do you think Lazarus and Mary play in the work of that faith community? What roles should they play?

2. Do you have siblings? Describe your relationship with them. If there are issues, what can you do to improve those relationships?

3. Why do you think Mary does not take on a leadership role? Do you know women who are reluctant to step

into leadership roles? How can you empower them to claim their rightful places of leadership?

4. How do you understand yourself as a leader? What enhances or hinders your leadership?

5. Martha is theologically astute; how does she display her knowledge in her conversation with Jesus? Why do you think the foundation of the church is based on Peter's confession of faith and not Martha's?

6. What is the difference between the faith stances of Martha and Mary? How are these differences reflected in their roles in the Luke text?

7. What in your life needs resurrection and new life? How are you praying about these concerns?

8. Do you identify more with Martha or Mary? Explain your answer.

9. How do you imagine the family dynamics changed once Lazarus was brought back to life?

10. Does the church effectively deal with matters of death and dying? Explain.

11

THE SAMARITAN WOMAN AT THE WELL

He Searched Me and Saw My Heart

READ

John 4:1–42

FOCUS TEXT

Then the woman left her water jar and went back to the city. She said to the people, "Come and see a man who told me everything I have ever done! He cannot be the Messiah, can he?" (John 4:28–29)

"So Jesus—do you want to go there? Go ahead, I can take it!" This unnamed woman is quite a character—at least, that is how she is portrayed in our traditional preaching and teaching. Her marital status is the focus, but there is so much more to her story than that. In fact, her conversation with Jesus is the longest one recorded in the Gospels. And theirs is no idle chitchat—they engage in a deep and wondrous the-

ological discussion. She asks questions and points out her understandings and Jesus seems genuinely intrigued by her. So delighted is he with her theological savvy, he discloses himself to her—he is the Messiah that the Jews have been anticipating. His disclosure deepens her belief, and she can't wait to go and tell others. She is the first evangelistic missionary! She is a foreign woman with a shady past, yet she is empowered to tell her story, and her entire village is convinced that Jesus is the Messiah.

Her story appears in the Gospel of John. As Jesus makes his way from Judea to Galilee, he takes the direct route through Samaria. Most pious Jews took the long way around to avoid being in Samaritan territory. The friction between the Jews and Samaritans is rooted in the political split of the nation of Israel after Solomon's death. The Northern tribes seceded from the nation and formed their own nation, keeping the name "Israel" and establishing their capital city at Samaria. The Southern tribes called their nation "Judah" and kept their capital city in Jerusalem. Both developed their own traditions, culture, and rituals, and felt superior to the other. Those in Jerusalem did not consider the Samaritans to be part of the house of Israel or of God's covenant with David. The Samaritans agreed with those in Judah that the Torah was the authoritative Word of God; but they worshiped on Mount Gerizim rather than Jerusalem. The Samaritans traced their ancestral roots to Joseph's sons Manasseh and Ephraim. The Samaritans were captured by the Assyrians in 721–22 BCE and scattered throughout the Assyrian empire. In addition, outsiders were imported to Samaria. The Samaritans intermarried with the Assyrians and others from Babylon, Syria, and other parts of the empire. For the Jews in Jerusalem, the Samaritans were a mixed breed of people who failed to keep ethnic purity. Therefore, they were unclean, and Jews were not permitted to interact with them. It is this division that gets played out in the

Gospels. Jesus's parable of the "good Samaritan" was a shocking story because, in the minds of the Jews, there was no such thing as a "good" Samaritan. When we learn that Jesus "had" go through Samaria, we are alerted that something momentous is about to happen.

Jesus sits by a well at high noon while his disciples go to find food. While he sits in the baking sun and scorching heat, a woman approaches the well. She immediately identifies him as a Jew. Proper protocol dictates that she not acknowledge or speak to him. But we know that Jesus hardly ever stood on protocol, and he asks the woman to give him a drink. Well, that's all she needs to launch into her story by making it clear that he has no business being there, no business speaking to her, and no business asking her for a drink of water from the well. That doesn't stop Jesus, and he tells her about living water. Whether she understands him or not is unclear; she points out, though, that he has no bucket to get any water, let alone living water. She understands that she cannot share water drawn with her bucket with him— the water would be unclean and he would be forbidden to drink it. Not only does she point out he doesn't have the necessary bucket, she asks who is he. The well was a gift from Jacob, one of the pillars of the faith—surely, Jesus does not think he is better than Jacob. In other words, even if he is a Jew, Jacob is one of his ancestors, too, and Jacob's water should be good enough for Jesus. In fact, the water from Jacob's Well was known to be refreshing and nourishing; the well reportedly never dried up even during droughts; it symbolized God's ongoing care and life-giving power for God's people—it, too, was a kind of living water. But Jesus continues his lesson on living water that quenches one's thirst for all time.

Perhaps it was his tone or his sincerity that convinced her that such living water was real—for she asks for some. Water that quenches thirst for all time would mean no more trips to the well for her, especially in the heat of the day. We cannot be sure whether she is serious or being sarcastic. Jesus, out of the blue, tells her to go and get her husband. She confesses that she is not married. Jesus knows this and tells her that the man she's with currently is not her husband. And this is where many stop with the story—imagine this woman who has had five husbands and is currently living with her boyfriend. This fact of her life raises questions— how is it that she's had five husbands? Did they die? Did they divorce her? Is she a victim of the levirate marriage tradition where a dead husband's brothers marry her so she can have a son? Is she a promiscuous harlot? None of these questions are answered by the text. Further, Jesus does not seem overly concerned about her marital status (nor does the biblical writer). Jesus doesn't pursue this matter and neither does the woman. Instead, she moves into a deeper theological issue—the true place of worship.

The place of worship is a sore point of contention between the Samaritans and the Jews. The Northern tribes felt that they had to find a place to worship other than Jerusalem. If the Samaritans tried to worship in Jerusalem, they would be rejected and some might defect to Judah. Therefore, the place of worship was religious as well as politically determined. Jesus tells the woman that God is not limited to a place—that God is a Spirit and should be worshiped in spirit and truth.

She continues to "wow" him with her theological understanding by stating that the Messiah is expected. God's Anointed One will make all things clear and plain—there won't be any more questions about how, when, and how to worship God; there won't be a divided nation anymore, all of God's people will be united once again. Jesus makes a startling declaration, "I am he, the one who is speaking to you." Jesus's self-disclosure is the first he makes using the formula, "I am" (in Greek, *ego eimi*), which establishes his identity with God. By stating *ego eimi*, Jesus connects himself with the God of the Hebrew Scripture, made known to the Israelites in their deliverance from bondage in Egypt. The divinity of Jesus is grounded in God; his humanity is centered in the incarnation—God's Word made flesh. His disclosure mirrors God's disclosure to Moses (see Exod.3:13–15).

At that moment, before she can react to this news, Jesus's disciples appear. They are astonished that he is talking to a Samaritan and a woman—but unlike the assertive and talkative woman, the disciples don't utter a word. While the disciples gather around Jesus, the woman does an astonishing thing—she leaves her water jar and runs into the city to tell others about her experience. Her message is simple, "Come and see!" She is clear that something wonderful has happened to her; but even in witnessing to her experience, she asks the pertinent question, "Can he really be the Messiah?"

Some scholars suggest that her question is one of doubt. Her faith, based on her experience, still brings questions. There is another way of reading her question, however—it can be one of incredulity, that is, "He can't really be the Messiah, can he?" If he is, this is powerfully good news, news almost too good to be true. Whatever her intentions with the question, her witness is enough to pique the interest of the others. We are not told whether her boyfriend is among those to whom she first testifies. Clearly, her marital situation is not important—her testimony is. So powerful is her witness, she convinces the others to gather at the well and implore Jesus to stay with them. He stays two days in a region where he wasn't even supposed to set foot. Many believed in him and witnessed firsthand the power of encountering Jesus.

Commentators have discounted the Samaritan woman's testimony by quoting verse 42 as proof that a woman's witness is not worthy of serious consideration. But the words of the townspeople serve to confirm the truth of faith—the witness of the community is important but also important is one's personal encounter with Jesus. In other words, faith is personal but not private. This echoes the testimony of John the Baptist—he knows Jesus is the One sent by God, but after his encounter, he knows for sure that Jesus is God's Anointed One—see John 1:32–34.

Huldah is the first biblical scholar and the unnamed Samaritan woman is the first biblical missionary for Jesus. This episode is found only John's Gospel; we know that the Johannine community embraced the Samaritans as full members of the faith community. In this story, the woman represents the Samaritans as those accepted and welcomed into God's household through their belief and faith in Jesus. Therefore, her name and marital status are secondary to her nationality. In embracing this woman, Jesus erases centuries of hostility and animosity towards the Samaritans. Again, we see Jesus crossing boundaries to draw people into his movement and into God's range of love, mercy, grace, and kinship.

This bad girl has a reputation to live down—the focus on her marital status and sexual history has been the grist for all kinds of judgmental teaching and sermons. But so little space is given to her personal life that we should get over it and move on. Her story is about spirituality and theology and not sexuality. She is portrayed as headstrong, theologically astute; she recognizes Jesus as a prophet and the Messiah and brings her entire village to Jesus and to faith in him. She leaves her water jars at the well just as the disciples left their nets and boats and families. The important thing she does is to tell others about her encounter and experience—she outs Jesus as the Messiah. She is an unlikely candidate for missionary work—she's a woman, a Samaritan, and may have a shady past—but she passionately shares her story about Jesus with others, who run with her back to the well where she has left her water jugs. In the heat of the day, the people, women and men, gather to listen to and learn from Jesus. The center of the Samaritan world shifts from Mount Gerizim to Jesus and God's realm, where there is grace for everyone.

At the beginning of her story, the biblical narrator states that the Jews and Samaritans share nothing in common. And now, they share Jesus! Jesus is for everyone—women, Samaritans, those with questionable virtue. In addition, her testimony permits us to question; doubts do not diminish God or God's power. God is not afraid of our questions. If Jesus is any indication, God welcomes them just as Jesus welcomes the questions of the woman.

We are cautioned by feminist and postcolonial scholars to be careful in how we interpret this story. The story does have imperialist implications—Jesus freely enters a forbidden territory; he parks himself by a well at high noon, a place where men do not generally gather. He expresses the superiority of his interpretation over the traditional renderings by both Jews and Samaritans. It is easy for Christians, especially in a postcolonial world, to be chauvinistic about our faith. It is important to respect the faith of others—it is one thing to share our testimonies and quite another thing to impose our understandings on others. We are cautioned to work towards decolonizing the world, to foster diversity and encourage pluralism, and to find ways to work in solidarity with those seeking liberation and freedom. We do not want to use the Bible or our faith to suppress others. The story of this bad girl, the Samaritan woman, is a cautionary tale that has the power to bring folks to Christ on their own terms and in their own ways.

REFLECTION QUESTIONS

1. How do you think the woman initially reacted to seeing Jesus sitting by Jacob's Well at noon? Do you think she was afraid to be alone with him?

2. Why do you think preachers and teachers have focused so much on the woman's colorful past? Why do you think the woman was drawing water at noon when there were no other women at the well?

3. How do you think her life changed after her encounter with Jesus? Do you think her testimony changed the way other Samaritans saw her?

4. Describe your experience of Jesus. That is, what is your testimony? Share as much as you feel comfortable doing.

5. Have you ever been defined by your gender or sexuality? In what ways? How did you handle the situation? What words of advice do you offer women who are sexually objectified?

6. Do you have any enemies? Who would consider you an enemy? Explain your answers.

7. What does "living water" mean to you? What in your life needs some living water? Explain.

8. Who are the "Samaritans" of our day? Why are they considered to be so? In what ways can you stand in solidarity with them?

9. How do you understand the connection between theology and mission? How does the church help or hinder effective missionary efforts?

10. What does the Samaritan woman teach you about witnessing and ministry? Explain.

12

MARY MAGDALENE
Were You There?

READ

Luke 8:1–3
John 20:1–18

FOCUS TEXT

Mary Magdalene went and announced to the disciples, "I have seen the Lord"; and she told them that he had said these things to her. (John 20:18)

"Yes, I was there from the beginning to the end. I went the distance with Jesus, no matter what!" There are so many legends surrounding Mary Magdalene that it is difficult to separate truth from fiction. We will try as we explore biblical references to her. She appears to be a leader of a band of women who follow Jesus and may be counted among his disciples. Further, she is the first to see the risen Christ and to tell about him. She plays an important role in the ministry of Jesus from its beginning to its glorious earthly end.

Tradition casts Mary Magdalene as a repentant sinner and former prostitute. There is, however, nothing in the Gospel texts that reasonably leads to that conclusion. Information about her is scant and, where there is little information, we are tempted to make up stuff. And that's what has happened to her. The portrait of Mary has been filled in by collapsing a number of biblical passages, most of which have nothing to do with her. Part of the confusion stems from the number of women simply identified as "Mary." Without other identifying information, it is not easy trying to figure out who's who, especially when unnamed women have been traditionally assigned the name "Mary Magdalene." In the Western Christian tradition, Mary Magdalene has been identified with the woman who weeps at Jesus's feet (Luke 7:36–50), the woman who anoints Jesus's body for burial (Mark 14:3–9, Matt. 26:6–13) and the woman caught in adultery (John 7:53–8:11)—but none of these are specified as Mary Magdalene.

Mary is identified not with a man but rather with a city. Magdala is thought to have been on the western side of the Sea of Galilee and north of Tiberias, a noted fishing town. She is one of many women from Galilee who join themselves to Jesus and his mission. She is listed, by name, in all four Gospels, although their treatment of her varies. In Luke 8:1–3, she is one of three named women (along with Joanna and Susanna) who lead many other women. Mary is always listed first to indicate her primary leadership role. It is believed that she and others represented a band of female disciples who shared in Jesus's inner circle of confidantes and disciples. At the very least, her presence indicates that Jesus was surrounded by a mixed group of disciples—females and males. It is refreshing to learn that Jesus valued the participation of women from the very beginning of his ministry—surely, these women heard Jesus's teachings and preaching, were sent out on mission projects, and were empowered to witness to the glory of God. Although we are not told the specifics of their work, we can assume that, as disciples, they participated in the same ways as did the twelve named male disciples. While it is refreshing for us to know that Jesus didn't exclude women because of their gender, their presence must have caused quite a stir among the people of his day. Jesus's itinerant ministry required a lot of travel and there in the midst of the men was a band of women!

We do not know the marital status of all these women; only Joanna is associated with a husband (Chuza) and we don't know if he is still living. The three named women and the others seem to be independent women, either single or widowed, who have the agency and resources to follow Jesus around. Married women were dependent on men for their financial livelihood and it would have been difficult for them to follow Jesus as he ministered in the countryside and in Jerusalem. Further, Mary Magdalene is said to be among those women who provided for Jesus and his mission from their own resources. There is some ambiguity about the nature and source of the resources the women provide. Some suggest that the women take on the domestic duties for Jesus and his disciples. The term used for service, *diakonia*, has a wide range of meanings, from "woman's work" of cooking and sewing, to table service, to the work of discipleship. It is not likely that Mary and her friends were domestic servants since Jesus's ministry is public and outside the private home. In addition, on more than one occasion, Jesus and the disciples are responsible for finding and providing food. And Jesus enjoyed home hospitality of a number of people throughout his travels. We cannot assume that the band of women who accompany Jesus just do "women's work."

It is also suggested that these women are former prostitutes and use their savings to finance Jesus's mission. Although prostitution was a lucrative "career" for women in ancient days, there is no indication of this choice for the

women who follow Jesus. Given the framework of patriarchy, we would expect any kind of unsavory background to
be highlighted. Instead, we are given no clues to the nature
or source of the women's resources. We conclude, then, that
these are women of some means (either through inheritance
or professional avenues) who are believers and wish to share
their time, talent, and monetary resources to support the
Jesus movement. The Greek word for resources used in Luke
is *hyparchontōn*, which usually means possessions, property, or money. We cannot categorically conclude that
women during Jesus's day had no financial resources—
clearly they did, and some used those resources to support
Jesus as part of their discipleship. We do not assume that
Jesus is a pimp who uses and exploits these women for his
own ends. Just as men hear Jesus's message about God's
reign and follow him, women also hear the message and are
converted to the work that Jesus embodies in his earthly
ministry and mission. These women are convicted with a
passion to do God's work and they have the means that
allow them, too, to follow Jesus. In Luke 8, we know that
the women have their own resources and that they control
those resources—they choose to share them with Jesus and
his other followers.

Mary Magdalene was a committed and faithful Galilean
disciple of Jesus. It is interesting to note that although women
were part of the Jesus movement, there are no recorded call
narratives, no recorded incidents of healing and preaching,
and no recorded public acts of ministry attributed to women.
We know, however, that they were around and they engaged
in ministry. It is suggested that Mary and the others participated out of thanksgiving for the healings enabled for them.
The only biographical information we have for Mary is
that she was sick with seven demons. In ancient days, all
manner of illnesses, physical and mental, were attributed to
demon possession. We are told that Jesus cast out the seven

demons plaguing Mary—she was really sick and became completely whole and well (the number seven signifies wholeness and completeness). But we do not know the motivation for the women's participation. It is just as likely that they responded as men did to the message of God's coming reign that Jesus preached.

In all four Gospels, Mary Magdalene is named among those who witness the crucifixion, burial, and resurrection of Jesus. There are some variations among the Gospels. In Mark, the women meet a stranger at the empty tomb. In Matthew and Luke, they experience an announcement of Jesus's resurrection. In John, Mary alone meets and talks with the resurrected Christ. Because it is the most detailed and shows the special relationship between Mary and Jesus, we will focus our attention to the resurrection appearances of Jesus in John.

In John, Mary Magdalene, always before in the text accompanied by other women, arrives at the tomb alone before dawn. She believes someone has snatched Jesus's body from the tomb when she finds that the stone covering the opening has been moved. She runs to inform Peter and the "beloved disciple"—this may be evidence of her leadership role in that she shares this distressing news with the known male leaders of the disciples. When she speaks, she does so as an insider by using the plural "we." Peter and the beloved disciple run to the tomb and find Jesus's burial clothes, suggesting that the body has not been stolen. The tomb is empty but there is not yet evidence of a resurrection. Mary returns to the story in verse 11—we presume she ran back to the tomb with the two disciples, but the text does not state this for sure. At any rate, she stands outside the tomb weeping. When asked why she is weeping, she expresses her personal grief at not knowing where Jesus is. The next voice is that of Jesus who repeats the question; again, she expresses her personal grief. There is great tension in this scene—we know something Mary doesn't—that it is Jesus now speaking to her. She assumes the one speaking to her is the gardener and she hopes he knows where Jesus's body is. Jesus reveals himself by speaking her name, "Mary!"

She then recognizes his voice and his presence. She uses a term of affection and intimacy in addressing him, *rabbouni*, which means rabbi, teacher, or master. Jesus reveals himself as the risen Christ to a woman, Mary, a woman who once was sick but now is well; once impaired, now whole; once on her own, now a disciple. Jesus does not simply reveal himself to her, he gives her a mission and a ministry—"go and tell the others that I am alive and well and ascending to heaven." Mary Magdalene has the distinction of being the first to proclaim the good news. She is the first to declare that Jesus has been raised and to proclaim his post-resurrection message of good news. Mary Magdalene, a woman once tormented by demons, is the first "Christian" preacher—spreading the good news that the Jesus movement has reached a new level. The others, including Peter, the beloved disciple, and the women, learn the reality of the resurrection from the witness of Mary. In John's Gospel, people bear witness to what they see, hear, and experience—Mary qualifies as a credible witness to the resurrected Christ.

Mary Magdalene is a bad girl who leaves her life to follow Jesus and gives generously of her resources to support his ministry and mission. We presume she is an intelligent, charismatic leader; sources beyond the Bible equate her leadership with Peter's and imply that she is the most knowledgeable of the disciples. She is identified as a serious conversationalist for Jesus and is spiritually insightful. She teaches the others when they are confused or puzzled by the words of Jesus. She enjoys a special relationship with Jesus—he calls her by name and appears to her first among his disciples. She is named, and all four Gospel writers recognize her leadership. In an age when women's participation in movements is limited and restricted to traditional women's work, Mary stands out as one who defies convention. When the other (male) disciples betray, deny, fall asleep, doubt and flee, Mary remains a constant in Jesus's life and ministry— he can count on Mary to be there, steadfast, unmovable. In an age when women's testimonies and witness are discounted and devalued as crazy ramblings, Jesus sends Mary to tell the others about God's glorious work in raising Jesus from the powers of death. In an age when men are held in higher esteem, Jesus commissions Mary to be his apostle and ambassador. While we do not have a full biographical picture of Mary Magdalene, we know her to be bold, articulate, loyal, passionate, persuasive, charismatic, competent, and intelligent. She is a pillar of faith and commitment and a role model for all disciples of Christ.

REFLECTION QUESTIONS

1. What leadership gifts do you think Mary Magdalene possesses? What do you suppose her leadership challenges might be?

2. It has been suggested that the seven demons that plagued Mary include jealousy, resentment, frustration, boredom, depression, and low self-esteem. What other "demons" might have tormented her? What "demons" are you struggling with?

3. How can women be empowered to claim their leadership gifts? How do you help or hinder other women's leadership?

4. What do you imagine Mary's relationship with Peter and the male disciples was like? What areas of friction do you imagine they encountered?

5. Despite her obvious importance to Jesus, why do you think Mary Magdalene disappears in the records of the early Christian movement and churches?

6. In what ways do you conform to traditional understandings of women's work and leadership? In what ways do you defy them?

7. How do you account for Mary's confusion about what has happened to Jesus when she arrives at the empty tomb?

8. In what ways is God calling life out of death throughout the world today?

9. How do you understand discipleship? In what ways do you share your resources on behalf of causes of justice and community?

10. What is the relevance of Jesus's resurrection today? What does Jesus command us to do today?

Preaching and Teaching
the Bad Girls

More Bad Girls of the Bible is designed to stimulate your curiosity and to send you on a path to further study. Good teaching and preaching seek to incorporate as many of our senses as possible—what do we see, hear, taste, feel because of our engagement with these stories? We don't have to be Egyptian slave women to feel unwanted and in the way. We don't have to be physically disabled to feel uncomfortable and shunned. So what can we do to bring these stories alive in real and embodied ways? We begin with a series of questions about the stories themselves. Then, we seek ways to embody them.

The challenge of teaching and preaching about women in the Bible is multilayered.

- There is a time lapse issue—concerns, rituals, cultural understandings, and political realities of ancient times differ from contemporary, postcolonial, postmodern realities. This gap must be accounted for so we don't ask the texts to answer questions they were not written to address. In addition, in the Gospels, we have to think about when the books were shaped—does the belief in the imminent second coming of Jesus factor into the way the stories are told? What is the relationship between the faith community and the Roman Empire? These and other questions must be considered.

- There is a language issue—the Bible is based on Hebrew, Aramaic, and Greek words, phrases, and syntax. We have to be careful when translating so that we don't infuse our understandings onto the texts.

- There is a cultural issue—the worldview of ancient peoples differs from our own. What makes sense to some of us—for example, marriages based on romance and love—would make little sense to ancient people. We must find ways to understand ancient culture and respect what we know of their ideas before we can find points of connection.

- There is a contextual issue—patriarchy is the overarching frame for the Bible and its myriad stories. Patriarchy does not value women beyond their roles as wives and mothers; so we can expect there to be tensions in the texts when we hold them up against contemporary realities. Women are objects of possession for men—their fathers, husbands, brothers, uncles, and sons. Further, the Bible is concerned more with public issues than private or domestic ones. So we don't have many stories dealing with women's feelings, reactions, and concerns except as they enhance or hinder men's stories. Then we must consider the context of the one who shapes the text. For example, the purpose of Mark's Gospel is to encourage a Gentile Christian community undergoing persecution; Luke's is an apologetic work to present Christianity as a nonthreatening community to the Romans; and John's focus is on Christology.

- There is a leadership issue—generally, women's roles are constrained and limited. Women who defy convention and step outside of prescribed roles either come to a bad end or are quickly put back in their place. Women, then, resort to deceit, seduction, and violence to exercise their power; notice that Rizpah resorts to a silent vigil to get her point across. Women's strategies are not often condemned in the Bible although they may raise questions for us.

- There is an ethical issue—the laws and regulations in the Bible highlight an ideal vision for community and life. Rarely are the laws a reflection of reality, but rather are held up as levels for which the people should be striving. What people do is placed against what they *should* do.

Feminist and womanist perspectives try to tease out some lessons from the texts. These methods take the stories of women seriously and are committed to highlighting the humanity and dignity of women and the worth of all human beings regardless of factors that impinge on their freedom. Feminist and womanist proponents seek to dismantle patriarchal attitudes and replace them with more egalitarian ones. Religious women believe that God takes up the causes of the poor and seeks to build a community of equals. This means deconstructing and reconstructing biblical narratives using various tools of interpretation in order to open up the texts to deeper, fuller, richer understandings.

Whether you are seeking ideas for teaching or preaching, consider the following questions to prime the pumps of your imagination and see where these bad girls take you:

1. What is the text saying? What are the details of the story? Who are the "characters" in the story?

2. What is the action of the story? What is the setting that has given rise to this particular text?

3. What is the challenge or conflict presented in the text? How is the challenge resolved?

4. Who speaks and who is silent? What do these actions mean?

5. What do we feel and think as we enact the story? What senses (sight, sound, smell, taste, etc.) are aroused by the text? What emotions are evoked?

6. What is God doing in the text? To what end does God act or not?

7. Are there any other biblical texts that relate to this particular text? Where? Under what circumstances are there connections?

8. What in the text is believable? What raises doubt?

9. Who in the Bible will disagree with this particular text? What would he/she say instead? Who in the church or community would disagree with this text? Why?

10. What can we learn from the story? How can we connect to the text today?

11. How does this text fit into God's wider purposes for creation and humanity? What does the text say about our lives and the world today?

12. What does the text call us to be or to do? What prevents us from fulfilling the text's call? What will happen if we fail to heed the text's call? What will happen if we fulfill the text's call?

In light of these questions and the answers that fit your context, I offer the following suggestions to get you started. I hope that the reflection questions for each unit serve to stimulate some thinking about how these stories can be used in the church. I am sure that you have some creative ways of preaching and teaching these biblical "bad girls."

HAGAR

- Imagine that Hagar and Sarah are on the "Dr. Joyce Brothers Show" where Dr. Brothers tries to bring some resolution to Hagar and Sarah's contentious relationship. Designate a person or persons to serve as Dr. Brothers, who has a set of questions to ask the women; Hagar, who answers out of her understanding of being exploited and abused by Sarah; and Sarah, who answers from a position of privilege and insecurity.

- Imagine that Ishmael and his stepbrother collaborate to write a Mother's Day tribute to Hagar. What will they say about her?

- In a sermon, convey the sense that God treats us like God treats Hagar—God seeks us, sees us, hears us, and provides for our needs.

- In a sermon, let us eavesdrop on a conversation between Eve and Hagar—what do they share about their lives and what do they share about God's dealings with them?

SHIPHRAH AND PUAH

- Imagine that Pharaoh has charged Shiphrah and Puah for crimes against the state because they refuse to kill Hebrew baby boys when they are born. Designate person(s) to serve as: a defense team for the women; a prosecuting team for Pharaoh; and witnesses for and against the women. Write a statement for each woman justifying her actions.

- In a sermon, talk about modern attempts to exterminate a particular group of people and how the midwives provide opportunities for hope, possibility, and promise in the midst of oppressive policies.

- In a sermon, construct a conversation between the midwives and Marian Wright Edelman, executive director of the Children's Defense Fund—what do they say to each other about their respective work?

MIRIAM

- Write a freedom song and choreograph a freedom dance by Miriam that will appear on YouTube. Have fun with this one!

- Construct a confrontation between Miriam and Moses's Cushite wife—what do they say to each other? Are they able to reconcile their differences? Remember that Miriam has a history of cooperating with women; have her explain her attitude toward her sister-in-law.

- In a sermon, highlight the importance of the performing arts in inspiring and sustaining hope for people engaged in the hard work of justice and liberation.

- In a sermon, talk about God's love of diversity and the need for us to deal with and overcome differences.

ZIPPORAH

- Imagine that Zipporah and Moses are appearing on "Divorce Court." Designate persons to be the judge, Zipporah, and Moses. What are the conflicts in their marriage? Why do they want a divorce? Is there the possibility for reconciliation?

- Imagine a conversation between Zipporah and her sisters. What does Zipporah share about her interracial-intercultural marriage to a murderer, fugitive from justice, and now liberator of the Hebrew people? What advice do they give their sister? What do they say about the children?

- In a sermon, talk about "circumcision" as a figurative way of cutting away the old things that hinder hope and obscure the future. Talk about what needs to be cut from our hearts, minds, and spirits so community can thrive and as a way of preparing for the new thing God is doing in the world.

BATHSHEBA

- Imagine that you are conducting premarital sessions for Bathsheba and David. Designate persons to represent the counselor, Bathsheba, and David. What questions do you wish to pose for them? How much of their past do you want them to reveal? How does each react to new knowledge about their intended? What issues do they bring to the marriage?

- Imagine a conversation between Bathsheba and her step-daughter, Tamar, who is raped by her half-brother, who is in turn killed by Tamar's brother. What of her experience does Bathsheba share? How does she comfort the girl? How does the girl react to Bathsheba's encounter?

- In a sermon, talk about what it means to raise a child of promise when the family situation is dysfunctional. Have Bathsheba consult the advice and wisdom of Sarah.

- In a sermon, focus on the grief of mothers—ancient and contemporary—whose children die prematurely. What supports do they need? What can the church offer them by way of support?

RIZPAH

- Imagine that Rizpah has been asked to deliver the keynote address for a conference on death and dying. What does she say? How much of her experience does she share? What resources does she offer for those gathered? Prepare a fifteen-minute speech.

- Imagine that Rizpah is a guest on "The Larry King Show." Designate persons to be Larry—what questions does he ask her? What do anonymous callers ask her about her life and her action? Does David call in to give his side of the story? Does she have an opinion about separation of church and state matters?

- In a sermon, let us eavesdrop on a conversation between Rizpah and Rosa Parks or some other freedom fighter. What do they say to each other about their stories, their strategies, and the outcomes of their subversive actions?

- In a sermon, provide a eulogy for Rizpah—what characteristics do you highlight about her life and her action on behalf of her slain family members?

HULDAH

- Imagine that Huldah is running for public office. Prepare a fifteen-minute speech in which she outlines her platform—what issues are important to her? What are her solutions to these issues? Where does she stand in relation to her political opponents?

- Imagine that her husband is being interviewed on MTV —what does he say about being "Mr. Huldah?" What concerns does he voice about his wife, her work, and their marriage?

- In a sermon, talk about social issues that need attention. What is God doing about these issues? What is God calling us to do and be concerning the issues you have identified?

- In a sermon, have Huldah and Amos talk about what God requires of us in working toward justice and community.

THE CRIPPLED/BENT-OVER WOMAN

- Imagine the crippled/bent-over woman has been asked to present a plan for universal health care. What concerns does she raise? What solutions does she propose?

- Imagine she has been asked to tell her story of healing. Prepare a five-minute "praise report" she will deliver at the annual Women's Day Service. What music, poems, or art will she include in her testimony?

- In a sermon, talk about the importance of forming coalitions and collaborative efforts to empower people to stand up under the burdens of injustice and oppression.
- In a sermon, construct a conversation between the woman and God—what do they say to each other? What does the woman say to God about her healing? How does God's grace continue to break through to help bent people stand tall and proud?

THE SYROPHOENICIAN WOMAN

- Create graffiti posters that contain affirmations about diversity and pluralism. Share the posters with other group members and post them around your church, if possible.
- Imagine the woman has been asked to speak at a fundraiser for the local women's shelter. What does the woman say? What of her experience does she share? What is her vision for the shelter?
- In a sermon, construct a communion liturgy where all are welcome to the table; or use your denomination's Eucharist service as the basis for your sermon.
- In a sermon, talk about the need to balance public work with private devotion—how does one care for others and care for self?

MARTHA AND MARY

- Imagine that Martha is the keynote speaker for a conference on women in the ministry. Prepare a fifteen-minute speech—what does she tell the women gathered? What struggles does she highlight and what advice does she offer them?
- Imagine that Mary has asked Dr. Phil to help her reconcile with her sister. Designate persons to be Dr. Phil,

Mary, Martha, and Lazarus. What do the siblings say to each other? What questions does Dr. Phil ask them? How do they react to each other? Do the sisters reconcile?

- In a sermon, talk about the importance of doing and hearing the word. Put Martha, Mary, and James in conversation with each other—what are the merits and challenges they present about ministry and mission?

- In a sermon, talk about the faith that continues to ask questions and even resist what is known about salvation and grace. Even after her confession of faith, Martha resists the life-giving and transformative power of Jesus—at Lazarus' tomb, Jesus asks the stone to be rolled away. Martha resists Jesus's intention to resurrect her brother—Lazarus is already dead for four days and the stench is overwhelming. Your sermon should focus on the stinkiness of life and those things that cause decay and Jesus's capacity and desire to bring life out of death. This sermon idea is based on the work of Adriene Thorne, Minister for Congregational Life at Middle Collegiate Church in New York City; she delivered her sermon at the Senior Chapel 2008 at Pacific School of Religion.

THE SAMARITAN WOMAN AT THE WELL

- Construct a template that can be transferred to Myspace or Facebook for the Samaritan woman. How much of her life does she post on the Internet? Who are the people she invites to be her "friends?" What does she want others to know about her?

- In a sermon, talk about what motivates people to leave their "water jars" to tell others about Jesus. Talk about this woman's evangelistic fervor and how we can capture that same spirit. Explain what such enthusiasm might do for church growth.

MARY MAGDALENE

- Imagine it is day one for Mary's new ministry; what is the topic for her sermon? What points does she want to make in her debut worship service?

- Mary has been asked to create a mentoring program for women in ministry. What concerns does she list as important? What advice does she offer these eager and talented women?

- Imagine a conversation between Mary Magdalene and Judas—what do they talk about? What advice does she offer him? Does he offer any advice to her?

- In a sermon, tell about Mary's obedience to Jesus's command to "go and tell" and its implication for our work on behalf of the church.

- In a sermon, let us eavesdrop on a conversation between Mary and Peter—as leaders of Jesus's movement, what do they say to each other? What challenges do they highlight about the other and about their mutual mission to continue Jesus's work on earth?

- In a sermon, talk about Mary's stewardship vision. In what ways does she encourage us to support the work and ministry of the church?

Well, these are some ideas to get you started. Please let me know how you use these stories in your ministry. Send your ideas and learnings to me or just drop a note to let me know what you are thinking on my website: www.barbara jessex.com. I look forward to hearing from you—and long live those "bad girls"!

RESOURCES/BIBLIOGRAPHY

ONLINE RESOURCES: MIDWIVES, DOULAS, AND CHILDREN

The Children's Defense Fund: www.childrensdefense.org.

O'Sullivan, Elizabeth. "The Turtle Women." Mothering. Issue 127, November/December 2004: http://www.mothering.com/articles /pregnancy_birth/midwives_doulas/turtle_women.html.

Pollon, Zelie. "The Legacy of Black Midwives." Mothering. Issue 144, September/October 2007: http://www.mothering.com/ articles/pregnancy_birth/midwives_doulas/legacy-of-black-midwives.html.

PRINT RESOURCES

Ackerman, Susan. "Why Is Miriam also among the Prophets? (and Zipporah among the Priests?)." *Journal of Biblical Literature* 121/01, 47–80.

Bach, Alice. *Women, Seduction, and Betrayal in Biblical Narrative.* Cambridge: Cambridge University Press, 1997.

Bird, Phyllis A. *Missing Persons and Mistaken Identities: Women and Gender in Ancient Israel.* Minneapolis: Fortress Press, 1997.

Blount, Brian K., ed. *True to Our Native Land: An African American New Testament Commentary.* Minneapolis: Fortress Press, 2007.

Brakeman, Lyn. *Spiritual Lemons: Biblical Women, Irreverent Laughter, and Righteous Rage.* Philadelphia: Innisfree Press, 1997.

Brenner, Athalya, ed. *Exodus to Deuteronomy: A Feminist Companion to the Bible.* 2nd ed. Sheffield, England: Sheffield Academic Press, 2000.

———. *I Am . . . Biblical Women Tell Their Own Stories.* Minneapolis: Fortress Press, 2005.

Bruce, Barbara. *Triangular Teaching: A New Way of Teaching the Bible to Adults.* Nashville: Abingdon Press, 2007.

Buchmann, Christina, and Celina Spiegel, eds. *Out of the Garden: Women Writers on the Bible.* New York: Fawcett Columbine, 1995.

Cartledge-Hayes, Mary. *To Love Delilah: Claiming the Women of the Bible.* San Diego: LuraMedia, 1990.

Davison, Lisa Wilson. *Preaching the Women of the Bible.* St. Louis: Chalice Press, 2006.

Doucet, Lyn Holley, and Robin Hebert. *When Wisdom Speaks: Our Living Experiences of Biblical Women.* Maryknoll, N.Y.: Crossroad, 2007.

Dube, Musa A. *Postcolonial Feminist Interpretation of the Bible.* St. Louis: Chalice Press, 2000.

DuBois, W. E. B. *The Souls of Black Folk.* New York: W.W. Norton, 1999.

Duran, Nicole Wilkinson. *Having Men for Dinner: Biblical Women's Deadly Banquets.* Cleveland: Pilgrim Press, 2006.

Essex, Barbara. *Bad Boys of the Bible: Exploring Men of Questionable Virtue.* Cleveland: Pilgrim Press, 2002.

———. *Bad Boys of the New Testament: Exploring Men of Questionable Virtue.* Cleveland: Pilgrim Press, 2005.

———. *Bad Girls of the Bible: Exploring Women of Questionable Virtue.* Cleveland: Pilgrim Press, 1999.

————. *Misbehavin' Monarchs: Exploring Rulers of Questionable Character*. Cleveland: Pilgrim Press, 2007.

Exum, J. Cheryl. *Fragmented Women: Feminist (Sub) Versions of Biblical Narratives*. Valley Forge, Pa.: Trinity Press International, 1993.

————. "Plotted, Shot, and Painted: Cultural Representations of Biblical Women." *Journal for the Study of the Old Testament. Supplement Series 215, Gender, Culture, Theory 3*. Sheffield, England: Sheffield Academic Press, 1996.

————. "Rizpah," *Word & World* 17/03 (Summer 1997), 260–68.

————. *Tragedy and Biblical Narrative: Arrows of the Almighty*. Cambridge: Cambridge University Press, 1992.

————. "You Shall Let Every Daughter Live: A Study of Exodus 1:8–2:10." *Semeia* 28/01, 63–82.

Gartner, Rosanne. *Meet Bathsheba: Dramatic Portraits of Biblical Women*. Valley Forge, Pa.: Judson Press, 2000.

Gench, Frances Taylor. *Back to the Well: Women's Encounters with Jesus in the Gospels*. Louisville: Westminster John Knox Press, 2004.

Hollies, Linda. *Sage Sisters: Essential Lessons for African American Women*. Cleveland: Pilgrim Press, 2008.

Hollyday, Joyce. *Clothed With the Sun: Biblical Women, Social Justice, and Us*. Louisville: Westminster John Knox Press, 1994.

Hoppe, Leslie J., O.F.M. *New Light from Old Stories: The Hebrew Scriptures for Today's World*. New York: Paulist Press, 2005.

Huwiler, Elizabeth. *Biblical Women: Mirrors, Models, and Metaphors*. Cleveland: United Church Press, 1993.

Kalas, J. Ellsworth. *Strong Was Her Faith: Women of the New Testament*. Nashville: Abingdon Press, 2007.

Kinukawa, Hisako. *Women and Jesus in Mark: A Japanese Feminist Perspective*. Eugene, Ore.: Wipf & Stock Publishers, 2003.

Klein, Lillian R. *From Deborah to Esther: Sexual Politics in the Hebrew Bible*. Minneapolis: Fortress Press, 2003.

McKenzie, Vashti. *Swapping Housewives: Rachel and Jacob and Leah.* Cleveland: Pilgrim Press, 2007.

Newsom, Carol A., and Sharon H. Ringe, eds. *The Women's Bible Commentary.* Louisville: Westminster John Knox Press, 1992.

Pearson, Helen Bruch. *Do What You Have the Power to Do: Studies of Six New Testament Women.* Nashville: Upper Room Books, 1992.

Porter, Jeanne. *Leading Ladies: Transformative Biblical Images for Women's Leadership.* Philadelphia: Innisfree Press, 2000.

Pui-lan, Kwok. *Postcolonial Imagination & Feminist Theology.* Louisville: Westminster John Knox Press, 2005.

Reid, Barbara E. *Choosing the Better Part? Women in the Gospel of Luke.* Collegeville: Liturgical Press, 1996.

Reis, Pamela Tamarkin. "Hagar Requited," *Journal for the Study of the Old Testament* 87 (2000), 75–109.

Robinson, Bernard P. "Zipporah to the Rescue: A Contextual Study of Exodus IV 24–6." *Vestus Testamentum* 36/04, (1985), 447–61.

Russaw, Kimberly D. "Zipporah and Circumcision as a Form of Preparation: Cutting Away at the Comfort Zone." *Journal of the Interdenominational Theological Center* 31/0102, 103–12.

Sakenfeld, Katharine Doob. *Just Wives? Stories of Power & Survival in the Old Testament and Today.* Louisville: Westminster John Knox Press, 2003.

Smith, Dennis E., and Michael E. Williams, eds. *The Storyteller's Companion to the Bible. Vol 13: New Testament Women.* Nashville: Abingdon Press, 1999.

Thockmorton, Burton H., Jr., ed. *Gospel Parallels: A Comparison of the Synoptic Gospels* 5th ed. Nashville: Thomas Nelson Publishers, 1992.

Thurston, Bonnie. *Women in the New Testament: Questions and Commentary.* New York: Crossroad Publishing, 1998.

Trible Phyllis, and Letty M. Russell, eds. *Hagar, Sarah, and Their Children: Jewish, Christian, and Muslin Perspectives.* Louisville: Westminster John Knox Press, 2006.

Weems, Renita J. *Just a Sister Away: A Womanist Vision of Women's Relationships in the Bible*. San Diego: LuraMedia, 1988.

Williams, Michael E., ed. *The Storyteller's Companion to the Bible: Old Testament Women*. Nashville: Abingdon Press, 1993.

Winter, Miriam Therese. *WomanWisdom: A Feminist Lectionary and Psalter, Women of the Hebrew Scriptures: Part One*. New York: Crossroad, 1991.

———. *WomanWitness: A Feminist Lectionary and Psalter, Women of the Hebrew Scriptures: Part Two*. New York: Crossroad, 1997.

———. *WomanWord: A Feminist Lectionary and Psalter: Women of the New Testament*. New York: Crossroad, 1990.